Leprosy in India: A Report
- Primary Source Edition

Timothy Richards Lewis, David Douglas Cunningham

CONTENTS.

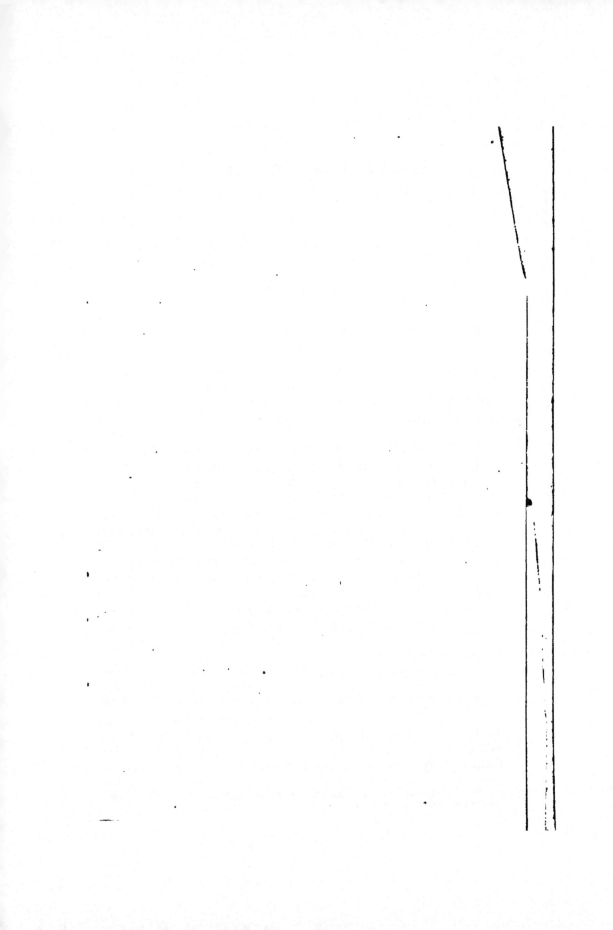

LEPROSY IN INDIA.*

T. R. LEWIS, M.B., AND D. D. CUNNINGHAM, M.B.

[REPORT I.]

INTRODUCTION:—THE DISTRIBUTION OF LEPROSY IN BRITISH INDIA.

IT is only within the last few months that it has become possible to obtain definite information regarding the local distribution and comparative prevalence of leprosy in the different districts of India. Now, however, that the Census Reports of 1872 have been issued, persons interested in the subject are in a position to form as correct an opinion regarding, not only the aggregate number of lepers, but also the distribution of the infirmity in India, as they are, probably, in almost any other country where leprosy prevails. In such a mass of figures it is doubtless probable that many errors have crept in, and that many persons have been registered as lepers who were not affected with true leprosy—notably such as are subject to that peculiar cutaneous affection characterised by more or less complete loss of pigment (*Leucoderma*). On the other hand, however, this excess may be balanced by the fact that quite as many, if not more, have been left out altogether.

No definite enquiry regarding the distribution of leprosy in India practicable until recently.

It is evident regarding the latter possibility, that as lepers formed one of the five classes of "infirmities" which were registered all over British India—the others being "Insanes," "Idiots," the "Deaf-and-dumb," and the "Blind"—persons may have suffered from leprosy for years without having been looked upon as

The "Infirmities" Tables of the 1872 Census Returns.

---

* Appeared as an Appendix to the *Twelfth Annual Report of the Sanitary Commissioner with the Government of India.*

lepers by the community, much less considered "infirm." The registration of some of the other "infirmities," such as dumbness and blindness, is not so liable to be affected by this manner of classification, although, even as regards such an infirmity as blindness, persons were not unfrequently returned in this category owing to their being possessed of but one eye. The want of more accurate definition was, probably, chiefly owing to the difficulty experienced in dealing with the different languages and dialects over such vast territories; in not a few cases, indeed, the expressions for some of the infirmities were found to have different significations in different parts of the same district.

Notwithstanding all this, however, the statistics are sufficiently exact with regard to such questions as the geographical prevalence of leprosy in this country to be of the utmost value, both to those who are engaged in the study of its causation, and to those who have been anxiously endeavouring to devise means for dealing with it in a practical manner.

We have gone over these figures very carefully, and have endeavoured to extract from them what appeared to us their most important features; we have also attempted to bring the returns of the different Presidencies and Provinces into such relation as to be fairly comparable. In some of the cases we have found considerable difficulty in doing so, owing to the great disproportion in the population of the areas which form the divisions, collectorates, and districts in the three Presidencies; for example, the population of a single division in Bengal—that of Burdwan—is equal to nearly half the population of the whole Presidency of Bombay. These we have attempted to correct as far as possible, and trust that a sufficiently succinct Tabular Statement of the distribution of the disease over British India has been devised to enable those interested in the question to estimate with a fair amount of accuracy the degree of its severity and the particular parts of the country specially affected.

Mode of procedure regarding the unification of the Returns of the different Presidencies.

In order still further to simplify this question, we have compiled a map of the disease as it is distributed over the country, which represents, graphically, the Tabular Statements gathered from the different censuses. The map has been very carefully compiled, and may be looked upon as representing in a fairly accurate manner the distribution of

The Leprosy-map of India.

the disease in accordance with the most recent official returns. Every district in the country was separately picked out on maps drawn on a large scale and tinted in accordance with the ratios found in the various columns in the original Census Reports, and the sheets were subsequently reduced to more portable dimensions. We have to acknowledge the great assistance which we obtained from Captain Waterhouse, Assistant Surveyor-General of India, in carrying out this scheme.

A glance at this map shows that there are three districts—large tracts of the country—where leprosy prevails to an extraordinary extent; namely, Beerbhoom and Bancoorah in the Burdwan division of Lower Bengal; the Kumaun division of the North-Western Provinces, extending across the southern range of the Himalayas; and the Deccan and Konkan divisions of the Bombay Presidency. The latter area, considered as a whole, does not show such an extreme prevalence as the two others : leprosy is, however, extremely prevalent, and in some districts, such as Barsi, Sowda, and Rajapur, abounds to a degree as great as is manifested in Beerbhoom, Bancoorah, and Kumaun.

TOTAL NUMBER OF LEPERS IN THE THREE PRESIDENCIES.

The accompanying summarised Tabular Statement shows that there are more than ninety-nine thousand leprous persons in British India alone, or at the rate of fifty-four cases in every hundred thousand of the population :—

The Summary Table.

TABLE 1.—*Showing the Number of Leprous Persons, and the Proportion in the Three Presidencies, together with the Total Population on which the Ratios have been calculated.*

	Total Population on which the Leper-ratios have been calculated.	Total Lepers.	Proportion of Lepers in every 10,000 [Ten Thousand] of the Population.
Bengal Presidency	135,456,138	71,287	5·2
Madras ditto	31,152,272	13,944	4·4
Bombay ditto	16,228,774	13,842	8·5
GRAND TOTAL IN BRITISH INDIA,	182,837,184	99,073	5·4

Of the three Presidencies, Madras, though not containing the fewest lepers, taking the absolute numbers, presents the lowest ratio, *viz.*, 44 to 100,000; whereas Bombay presents a proportion of leprous population nearly double that of Madras—85 lepers to every 100,000, although the absolute number of lepers in the Bombay Presidency is slightly fewer. The Presidency of Bengal furnishes an intermediate proportion—very considerably lower, however, when the whole Presidency is considered, than that of Bombay. The figures in the following Table, however, point to the fact that one of the divisions in Bengal (Burdwan) contains a greater proportion of lepers, and absolute numbers almost as great as those of the whole of the Bombay or Madras Presidency.

The Detailed Table.

In Table II will be seen the figures giving the total numbers of lepers recorded in the Census Returns of this country, but on the present occasion it will be sufficient to refer to them collectively, for the most part, as it will be more convenient to examine them categorically on a future occasion.

TABLE 2.—*Showing the Distribution of Leprosy in British India.*

	Divisions.	Total number of Lepers.	Proportion of Lepers in every 10,000 [Ten Thousand] of the Population.		Divisions.	Total number of Lepers.	Proportion of Lepers in every 10,000 [Ten Thousand] of the Population.
BENGAL.				**OUDH.**			
BENGAL PROPER	Burdwan	12,091	16·5		Lucknow [Unao District in]	650	7·0
	Presidency	3,682	5·6		Rae Bareli	?	
	Rajshahye	6,182	6·9		Fyzabad	?	
	Cooch Behar	244	5·7		Seetapur [Hurdul District in]	688	7·0
	Dacca	5,299	5·5		ESTIMATED TOTAL	7,831	7·0
	Chittagong	915	2·6				
	TOTAL	28,403	7·8	**BERARS.**			
BEHAR	Patna	5,742	4·3		Berars	1,432	6·0
	Bhaugulpore	2,031	3·0				
	TOTAL	7,773	3·9	**CENTRAL PROVINCES.**			
ORISSA.	Orissa	1,077	2·4		Nagpur	892	4·0
					Jubbulpore	137	1·0
CHOTA NAGPORE	Chota Nagpore	567	2·6		Narbada	552	3·0
					Chattiagarh	1,216	4·0
ASSAM.	Assam	309	1·6		Upper Godavari	10	1·0
					TOTAL	2,807	3·0
	GRAND TOTAL IN PROVINCE	38,129	5·4	**PUNJAB.**			
					Delhi	1,273	6·6
NORTH-WESTERN PROVINCES.					Hissar	605	4·9
					Umballa	1,524	9·2
	Meerut	1,463	2·9		Jullundur	2,758	11·1
	Rohilcund	2,256	4·2		Amritsar	1,774	6·4
	Agra	1,145	2·3		Lahore	633	3·3
	Jhansie	211	2·3		Rawalpindi	1,613	7·3
	Allahabad	1,828	3·3		Mooltan	452	3·0
	Benares	1,625	2·0		Derajat	153	1·5
	Kumaun [with Garhwal]	1,571	21·0		Peshawar	204	1·9
					TOTAL	10,989	6·2
	TOTAL	10,099	3·3		GRAND TOTAL IN BENGAL PRESIDENCY	71,287	5·2

TABLE 2.—*Showing the Distribution of Leprosy in British India*—concld.

	Districts.	Total number of Lepers.	Proportion of Lepers in every 10,000 [Ten Thousand] of the Population.	Divisions.	Collectorates.	Total number of Lepers.	Proportion of Lepers in every 10,000 [Ten Thousand] of the Population.
	MADRAS.				**BOMBAY.**		
SEA COAST DISTRICTS	Ganjam	698	5·0	DECCAN.	Khandesh	1,532	15·0
	Vizagapatam	586	4·0		Nasik	718	10·0
	Godavari	654	4·0		Ahmadnagar	1,085	14·0
	Kistna	517	4·0		Poona	1,090	12·0
	Nellore	545	4·0		Satara	1,321	12·0
	Madras	418	10·5		Sholapur	795	12·0
	Chingleput	580	6·0		Belgaum	943	10·0
	South Arcot	849	5·0		Dharwar	1,155	12·0
	Tanjore	1,430	7·0		Kaladgi	607	7·0
	Madura	659	3·0		TOTAL	9,246	11·6
	Tinnevelly	810	5·0				
	Malabar	1,378	6·0	KONKAN.	Kanara	158	4·0
	South Canara	748	8·0		Ratnagiri	1,237	12·0
					Kolaba	444	12·6
	TOTAL	9,872	4·9		Bombay	209	3·0
					Tanna	705	8·0
					TOTAL	2,753	8·4
				GUJERAT.	Surat	579	10·0
					Broach	188	5·0
INLAND DISTRICTS.	Kurnool	349	4·0		Kaira	411	5·0
	Cuddapah	405	3·0		Panch Mahals	114	5·0
	Bellary	631	4·0		Ahmedabad	242	3·0
	North Arcot	1,253	6·0		TOTAL	1,534	5·4
	Salem	554	3·0				
	Coimbatore	399	2·0				
	Nilgiris	41	8·0				
	Trichinopoly	343	3·0	SIND.	Kurrachee	81	2·0
	Puducottah Territory	97	3·0		Haidarabad	126	2·0
					Thar and Parkar	8	?
	TOTAL	4,072	3·6		Shikarpore	87	1·0
					Upper Sind Frontier	7	1·0
					TOTAL	309	1·4
	GRAND TOTAL	13,944	4·4		GRAND TOTAL	13,842	8·5

With regard to the portions of the Table that refer to the Punjab, Oudh, and the Be-

Imperfect information regarding the Punjab, Oudh, and the Berars.

rars, it is to be remarked that the statistical details are not so fully given as in other parts of the country, so that we have been compelled to resort to such official documents as we could procure other than the local Census Reports. In arranging the Leper Returns for the Punjab, for instance, we have made use of some valuable data which its Sanitary Commissioner, Dr. D'Renzy, had collected; and the figures regarding leprosy in the Berars were obtained from the Oudh Census Report published in 1869. Unfortunately when the census of Oudh itself was taken, the leper population was ascertained in only one district, Hurdui, so that merely an estimate of the aggregate number can be submitted. During the present year, however, another district has been registered, that of Unao, and this gives a proportionate result precisely corresponding with that registered on a former occasion.

With these exceptions, the figures in the Table have been derived from the original census records as published by the various local Governments.*

THE LOCALITIES IN WHICH LEPROSY IS EXCEPTIONALLY PREVALENT.

It may be useful to indicate, generally, in what parts of the country leprosy is exception-

Localities where Leprosy is specially prevalent.

ally prevalent, so that the attention of observers who may happen to reside in such localities may be arrested; and it is hoped that they may be thus induced to take a special interest in the endeavour to elucidate some peculiarities which the district or its inhabitants may present when carefully searched after. It is obvious that over such a vast area very small communities cannot be thought of in a general review, so that, perhaps, for the purpose of the present report, it will be sufficient to select such districts or tracts of country as are exceptionally unfortunate in this respect, which contain not fewer than, say, 100,000 souls. It may be assumed that a locality with such a population and with a proportion of lepers equivalent to 20 per 10,000—that is to say, of 1 leper to every 500 persons—

---

* In some of the Census Reports the nearest whole numbers have been given instead of the decimal fraction.

is deserving of very special attention, not only for the study of the disease, but also for the purpose of devising some means whereby the troubles of the unfortunate sufferers may be mitigated.

We have therefore carefully examined the returns with the object of being able to bring into prominent notice all the larger districts in the three Presidencies which are burdened with such a high proportion of lepers as 2 per 1,000 implies, and have arranged the data thus collected into the subjoined Tabular Statement:

TABLE 3.—*Districts of* 100,000 *Inhabitants and upwards which contain a Leprous Population equivalent (or nearly so) to* 20 *per* 10,000.

Presidency.	Division or Collectorate.	District, &c.	Population of District, &c.	Total Lepers in District, &c.	Lepers per 10,000 of Population of District, &c.
Bengal ...	Burdwan ...	Beerbhoom ...	695,921	2,872	41·2
Ditto ...	Ditto ...	Bancoorah ...	526,772	1,578	30·0
Ditto ...	Ditto ...	Burdwan ...	2,034,745	4,604	22·6
Ditto ...	Kumaun ...	Kumaun & Garhwal	743,602	1,571	21·1
Ditto ...	Allahabad...	Banda * (Tehseel)...	108,771	214	19·6
Ditto ...	Meerut ...	Dehra Doon ...	115,771	220	19·0
Bombay	Sholapore ...	Barsi ...	130,853	335	25·6
Ditto ...	Khandesh ...	Sowda ...	124,519	312	25·0
Ditto ...	Ratnagiri ...	Rajapore ...	168,498	395	23·4
		TOTAL ...	4,649,452	12,101	26·0
Madras	The highest district is that of Madras itself, 10·5 per 10,000.				

* Girwain (population 78,848), in Banda District, contains 40 lepers per 10,000.

The foregoing numerical data regarding the distribution of leprosy in British India can, as already stated, be accepted as only approximately correct so far as the actual enumeration of the lepers is concerned, but what is probably of considerably more importance in connection with the study of its etiology is, that they convey fairly accurate information regarding the particular parts of the country where the disease is most prevalent. This

The relative value of the numerical and geographical data.

is, we believe, the first attempt that has been made, or could have been made, with any prospect of accuracy, seeing that some of the most important census papers have only very recently been issued, to map out the distribution of leprosy over the Peninsula. Unfortunately, the large portion of the country which is not directly under British control must remain still undescribed. It is known to prevail in many of the districts under native rule to a very great extent, but that is all that can be said.*

THE FORMS OF LEPROSY ENCOUNTERED IN INDIA, AND THE DESIGNATIONS APPLIED TO IT BY THE PEOPLE.

As regards the forms of leprosy that are met with in this country, they may, we think,

The forms of Leprosy encountered in India.

be classified very conveniently under the two headings generally adopted by modern writers—a classification based on the two most characteristic features of the disease. These features it will be more convenient to describe when the result of clinical observations come to be recorded; in the meantime it will be sufficient to mention generally what these leading characteristics are. In one form the most prominent feature con-

The "Anæsthetic" and "Tubercu-lated" Leprosy.

sists in the diminished sensibility manifested over various parts of the body, and it has consequently been designated the anæsthetic form—*Lepra anæsthetica*—induced, it is believed, by a peculiar alteration in the cutaneous nerves of the part. The other leading form is commonly referred to as the tuberculated variety— *Lepra tuberculosa*—characterised by analogous changes in the skin and in other tissues, so that the parts in question

---

* Whilst this Report was being printed, we had the opportunity of consulting the recently-published "Report on the Census of British Burma," from which we extract the following data regarding the number and distribution of lepers in that Province:—

BRITISH BURMA.						
Division.				Population.	Number of Lepers.	Lepers per 10,000 of Population.
Arakan	...	...	...	...	484,362	185	3·8
Pegu	...	...	...	...	1,662,058	2,072	12·4
Tenasserim	...	...	...	...	600,727	946	15·7
		TOTAL	...	2,747,148	3,203	11·6

B

present more or less tuberculated, nodular projections of various sizes and outline.

The existence of the two forms in one person forms the third, mixed variety, of some writers, but, as Virchow says, "no clear line of demarcation exists between the nervous and cutaneous forms of leprosy." We hardly think it necessary, therefore, to adopt this term as distinctive of any particular form of the disease, seeing that at best the terms "Anæsthetic" and "Tuberculated" are only used relatively according as the one or other feature characterises the phase of the malady most prominently. At the same time, in some instances the two symptoms are so equally evident, that it is difficult or impossible to classify them satisfactorily, and in such a case the designation "mixed" variety may be conveniently resorted to. For convenience of description, a fourth term may be adopted, as suggested by Dr. Vandyke Carter, to designate those cases in which the eruption forms the most prominent characteristic. These two may be looked upon as *varieties*. The eruption may constitute a conspicuous feature in either the anæsthetic or the tuberculated form.

The subordinate classes of Leprosy,—the "Mixed" and "Eruptive."

The terms applied by the various populations of India to indicate the disease are not so numerous as might have been expected, considering the number of languages and dialects there are in the country. Although the works on medicine which the *hakeems*, or native practitioners, consult, recognise at least eighteen varieties of the disease, the ordinary native only recognises one or two general terms for the complaint. This seems to be due chiefly to the fact that the principal ancient treatises on medicine in this country were written in Sanskrit—a circumstance which accounts for the general uniformity in the terms adopted for the leading diseases in the different provinces. Indeed, it is probable that, with regard to leprosy, most natives in any part of India would understand what was referred to from the Sanskrit *Kushtha*, or some of its vernacular forms, such as *Kushta* (Teligu and Tamil) Kúth or *Kút* (pronounced *Koot*) or *Kúd* (Bengali, Uriyá and Assamese) and *Kút* or *Korh* (Hindi, Punjabi and Marhatti). By way of euphemism the disease is also commonly indicated by the Sanskrit terms *Roga* (vernacular *Rog* pronounced *Rogue*) and *Vyádhi* (vernacular

The names by which Leprosy is known all over India.

Byádh—both meaning "disease") or *Mahárog* or Mahá-byádh, "the great disease." The Arabic term *Juzám** is likewise extensively used in Northern India, and rarely, the Persian *Luri*. These terms are generally applied to the tubercular forms of leprosy, or rather to the forms character-ised by the presence of deformities; whereas the more distinctly anæsthetic form is frequently described as *Sun-bharri* (deprived of sensibility, Hindee). The Arabic word *Baras*, the Persian *Pes* and the Sanskrit *Dhaval* (white) are also used to designate leprous conditions, but generally these terms refer to an affection which is not leprous, *viz.*, the albino-condition of the skin described by systematic writers as *Leucoderma*—a circumstance which, as already mentioned, very greatly enhances the difficulty of obtaining correct statistics regarding leprosy proper.†

The disease has been known to exist in India for at least

Leprosy in ancient India. ‡ 3,000 years, but comparatively little was definitely known regard-ing its localisation in the various parts of the country until the

---

* *Juzám* is explained in the Arabic dictionaries as "a certain disease arising from the spreading of the blackbile, throughout the whole person, so that it corrupts the tempera-ment of the members, and the external condition thereof and sometimes ending in the corrosion, or falling off, of the members, in consequence of ulceration."

† Dr. Rájendralála Mitra, the well-known Sanskrit scholar, has very kindly, revised the above paragraph.

‡ The " Proceedings of the Asiatic Society of Bengal" for August 1875 (page 160) contains a very interesting communication by Bábu Rájendralála Mitra, LL.D., in reply to some questions regarding Leprosy in Ancient India put to the Society by Dr. W. Munroe. Dr. Mitra writes :—

" Taking Sus'ruta to be 400 B. C. (this date is Wilson's, I take him to be two centuries older) we must look for the date of Charaka, whom he quotes, in the sixth century B. C. Sus'ruta professes to record the lectures of his tutor Dhanvantari, and very sparingly quotes his predecessors ; but his chapter on Leprosy is founded on Charaka, as Dr. Munroe will easily perceive by comparing Hesseler's translation in Latin (published at Leipzig) with the enclosed from Charaka, which I have got prepared from him. In Sus'ruta's time Charaka was an old authority of great weight, and an interval of two centuries between the two is by no means an extravagant guess. Now Charaka quotes Átreya, who was a son of Atri, a sage of great renown, who is named in the Vedas, and was the author of one of our text-books on Law. The name of Átreya occurs in Pánini, whose date Goldstücker takes to be the 9th century B. C. It is also met with in the Rig Veda Sañhitá, which dates from the 14th century B. C. Charaka also quotes Bágbhata, who, likewise, has a chapter on Leprosy. Bágbhata, again, quotes Agnivesa, who was a great grammarian, and is named in the Madhukánda of the S'atapatha Bráhmana of the White Yajur Veda, and Játukarna, who is named in the Yájñavalkya Kánda of the same Veda. The works of the last two are lost, but on the authority of Bágbhata we may fairly accept them to have been professors of medicine, though it is impossible to say whether they wrote on Leprosy or not. Manu mentions Leprosy, but the recension of Manu we now have is supposed to be not older than the 6th century B. C. In Sus'ruta's work the word *Kushtha*, the Sanskrit name for Leprosy, has been used in a generic sense, and includes several cutaneous diseases which are not leprous, but from Átreya's descriptions quoted by Charaka, it is evident that the word primarily meant Leprosy. It does not occur in the Rig Veda Sañhitá, which dates from the 15th century B. C., and if we could accept this negative evidence to be of any weight, we could say that the disease was not known in the 15th century ; but as there is no reason why the name of a disease should occur in a book of hymns, it is of no value; while the name of Átreya, which occurs in that Veda, and has been cited as that of an authority on the

results of the censuses of 1872 had been published. Very important advances have within the last few years been made in the acquisition of knowledge regarding the pathology of leprosy, and it will be our duty in a future report to describe these very fully; but with regard to our definite knowledge of its actual causation, it is to be feared that we have not, except phraseologically, advanced very much on the etiological views recorded by Atreya many centuries B. C., which were to the following effect: " When the seven elements of the body become vitiated through the irritation

---

subject, would carry us much beyond the 13th century B. C., to which Dr. Munroe limits the enquiry.

" Extract from the Charaka Sáñhitá on the Pathology of Leprosy.

" Átreya says—' When the seven elements of the body become vitiated through the irritation of the wind, the bile, and the phlegm, they affect the skin, the flesh, the spittle, and the other humours of the body. These seven are the causes respectively of the seven varieties of *Kushtha*. The *Kushthas* thus produced cause much pain and suffering. None of these varieties results, however, from the vitiation of a single humour. *Kushthas* are of seven, of eleven, or of a larger number of kinds ; and these, constantly irritating the system, become incurable.' We shall give a brief account of these as they are produced by the vitiation of the different humours. The wind, the bile, and the phlegm, being vitiated, react on the skin, &c. When the wind is most vitiated it produces the *kapála kushtha*, the bile the *audumbara*, the phlegm the *mandála*, the wind and the bile the *rishyajihvá*, the bile and the phlegm the *paundarika*, the phlegm and the wind the *sidhma*, and the three together the *kákanaka*.

" Excessive physical exercise after exposure to too much heat or too much cold ; taking food after surfeit ; eating of fish with milk ; using barley and several other grains, such as *hayanaka, dalaká, kurodusá,* &c., along with venison, milk, curdled milk, and buttermilk ; excessive sexual intercourse ; long-protracted excessive fear or labour ; fatigue, interruption of catarrh, &c.,—vitiate the phlegm, the bile and the wind ; hence the skin and the three others become slackened. Thus irritated, the three elements corrupt the skin and others, and produce *kushtha.*

" The premonitory symptoms of *kushtha* are as follow : Want or excess of perspiration, roughness, discolouration, itching and insensibility of the skin, pain, horripilation, eruptions and excessive pain on the parts that are about to fall off.

" Some *kushtha* eruptions are red, rough, spreading and small ; they cause horripilation, slight itching, pain, and discharge of matter and sanies. These are caused by wind, and are called *kapála-kushtha* (scaly).

" Those that are of a coppery colour, which discharge matter, blood and sanies, cause itching pain, inflammation and burning, and produce worms, are also caused by wind. They appear like the ripe fig, and are hence called *Audumbara* (fig-like).

" Some are cold to the touch, raised, hard, reddish-white, clammy, itching and infested with worms. These, too, are caused by wind ; they are called *Mandala* (circular).

" Those which are rough, red, white, yellow, blue or coppery, producing itching pain, worms, burning sensation, and insensibility, are also caused by wind. They have the appearance of the tongue of an antelope, and are hence called *Rishyajihva.*

" Those which are white or red, spreading and elevated ; which discharge blood, pus and sanies, and produce itching, are also caused by wind. They appear like the leaves of the white lotus, and hence are called *Paundarika.*

" Those that are rough, red, thin, internally cold, sometimes reddish-white, which cause slight pain, itching, burning, and discharge of pus and sanies, are also caused by wind. They appear like the flowers of the pumpkin, and are called *Sidhma.*

" *Káknaka* and others have all the symptoms of *kushtha*. They are incurable, while the others are curable. That which is incurable can never be cured, and those which are curable sometimes become incurable.

" The wind causes coppery-red roughness, pain, inflammation, shrinking, horripilation, and insensibility of the skin. The bile produces burning, perspiration, pain, discharge of blood, and suppuration. The phlegm causes whiteness, coldness, itching, and confluent pimples.

of the wind, the bile and the phlegm, they affect 'the skin, the flesh, the spittle, and the other humours of the body. These seven are the causes respectively of the seven varieties of *Kushtha*" (leprosy).

" The worms that form in leprous eruption destroy the flesh, skin, veins, muscles and bones. When affected by them, the patient suffers from spontaneous discharges of blood, insensibility, loss of sensibility of the skin, mortification, thirst, fever, dysentery, burning, weakness, disrelish and indigestion. Then *kushtha* becomes incurable. The man who neglects the disease at its commencement is sure to die. He, who at the first breaking out of the disease tries to get rid of it, may be sure of its being cured."

LEPROSY, AS OBSERVED IN KUMAON.

IN accordance with instructions which we received from the Government of India, we proceeded to Almora, the headquarters of the Kumaun and Garhwal Division, early in May last, for the purpose of commencing a series of systematic observations regarding leprosy. The Commissioner, General Sir Henry Ramsay, had specially addressed the Lieutenant-Governor of the North-Western Provinces, pointing out the urgency of such an investigation, and strongly recommending the Kumaun district as peculiarly adapted for its prosecution. General Ramsay writes in May 1875 : "It would be impossible to find anywhere in India so suitable a locality as Kumaun for pursuing a thorough and complete investigation into the whole subject of leprosy. At Almora we have an asylum containing on an average 100 lepers, labouring under every form and stage of the disease, whose family history can be ascertained to the minutest detail. In the district there are many hundreds either wandering alone as beggars or residing at their homes, whose history could be gathered with perfect accuracy. Such a record would give a mass of statistics which would admit of some reliable deductions being drawn, as to whether it is possible to deal with this loathsome disease. In my opinion it is necessary that something should be attempted. If, on inquiry, it is found that nothing can be done, then it will be so far satisfactory to have ascertained that as a fact; but in the absence of that knowledge it appears to me wrong that this fearful disease should be allowed to continue to spread itself amongst the population if any measures can be taken to prevent it." In this the Lieutenant-Governor, Sir John Strachey, coincides, and adds that "the field of inquiry, while sufficiently large, will not be unmanageable in extent."

Sir Henry Ramsay on Leprosy in Kumaun.

Writing in 1874 to the India Office, the Army Sanitary Commission, in reiterating its suggestion that the whole subject of leprosy should be examined in India, says :—" The first step towards this examination is to obtain accurate statistics

The Army Sanitary Commission's and Dr. Gavin Milroy's suggestions.

of the disease, such as can show not only the usual numerical data, but the precise localities where leprosy exists in India." And Dr. Gavin Milroy, who probably has a more extensive and accurate knowledge of the malady and its literature than any other writer in England, remarks, in a communication regarding the manner in which in his opinion the present inquiry should be conducted, as follows : "Commencing, therefore, as if the subject were a *tabula rasa*, Drs. Lewis and Cunningham will first make themselves acquainted with the natural history of the disease as it occurs in Hindustan; its essential and pathognomonic outward and physical symptoms; the circumstances and conditions which influence its origination and spread; the factors which seem to affect or modify its progress, whether beneficially or otherwise, apart from direct medication or the action of drugs, internal or external—in short, all its characteristic features and attributes. They will thus determine the general nosological nature of the malady, and whether Cullen has rightly classed it as a '*cachexia totius vel magnæ partis corporis habitus depravatus, sine pyrexia primaria vel neurosis*;' and the College of Physicians ranged it among the 'General Diseases' between Lupus and Scrofula."

We have on the present occasion endeavoured to follow out the preliminary stages of these suggestions so far as was compatible with the circumstance that, owing to the advent of the rains in July and the consequent difficulty in getting about among the hills, it was not deemed advisable to undertake any systematic personal investigation of the special localities in which the disease prevails, during the current year. This part of the inquiry we hope to be in a position to be able to report upon on a future occasion. At present we purpose restricting our remarks to such portions of the inquiry as may be comprised under the following heads :—

Nature of the present series of investigations.

A—Analysis of the Statistics of the District.

1. To what extent does leprosy prevail in Kumaon?
2. Is the disease exceptionally prevalent in this district?
3. The geographical distribution of the disease in the district.
4. What are the main features in connection with the localities in which it most prevails?

B—Analysis of the Statistics of the Almorah Leper Asylum, and of the results of Clinical observations.

1. Number of lepers admitted since the Asylum was founded, and the more prominent facts concerning them generally.
2. Clinical observations regarding the persons affected with anæsthetic leprosy; 3, Tuberculated leprosy; 4, Mixed varieties of leprosy; and 5, The so-called eruptive varieties of leprosy.
6. Analysis of all the cases and deductions regarding the influence of age, sex, predisposition, &c., in the etiology of the disease.

A—Analysis of the Statistical Records regarding Leprosy in Kumaun,

1.—To what extent does the disease prevail in the district?

BEFORE submitting the figures regarding the distribution
of leprosy in Kumaun, it will be
The District of Kumaun: Its posi-
tion geographically. advantageous to have a general
idea of the principal physical
features of the territory under consideration. The district
forms a part of the North-Western Provinces, and extends
in a north-easterly direction from the plains across the
Southern Himalyan range to the borders of the Ari province
of Tibet, and the central range. It is separated from Nepal
on the east by the Kali River, and the District of Garhwal
forms its western boundary, the extreme points which it
touches being 29° 5'—31° 6' north latitude, and longitude
78° 17'—80° 5'. It extends over an area of about 7,000
square miles—an area nearly as extended as the whole of
Wales.

It has been truly stated that no country exhibits more
extraordinary diversities of ele-
Physical features. vation, temperature, and climate
than Kumaun. With the exception of the low marshy
land or terai which extends along its southern part, it con-
sists for the most part of a series of mountains, some of
which are among the loftiest in the world. Crystalline schists
constitute the prevailing geological features. The mountains
do not form a continuous ridge, but a series of hills separated
by deep valleys, along which torrents and rivers course, and
ultimately discharge themselves into the Ganges and Gogra.
No single temperature-chart of this district could be of value,
seeing that the variations in its different localities are so
very marked, as may indeed be inferred from the fact that
there are, it is said, some thirty-four hills within its borders
whose summits reach to 18,000 feet and upwards; consequently every range of temperature is to be found, from the
tropical heat of the terai and the deep valleys, to an almost
arctic cold.

Previous to the year 1815 the district was under native
rule, but for the last sixty years
Its political history and inhabitants. it has formed a portion of the
British dominions. The inhabit-
ants are for the most part of Hindu origin, but towards the
northern extremity of the country they are of Tartarian

c

descent, and are known as Bhotias. The latter inhabit principally the slopes of the snowy range. Practically there are, besides the Mahomedans, only two castes to be found in Kumaun—Rajputs and Domes. The former, constituting the upper classes of the community, are engaged for the most part in agricultural pursuits, and the latter act as menials or carry on such trades as are considered of an inferior kind.

The habits of all classes alike are, as among most hill people, exceedingly filthy, and their villages in great part are devoid of any attempt at the observance of the ordinary rules of public health. Man and beast live in the same dwelling all the year round, the ground floor of nearly all the houses being occupied by cattle, sheep, and goats. That dirt, however, is of itself sufficient to induce leprosy, is strongly contraindicated by the fact that the Bhotias who inhabit the northern parts of Kumaun are even dirtier than their Kumaunee brethren. It is said they never wash, such an act being considered by them as one certain to be followed by some grievous misfortune, and yet they are, we are informed, practically free from leprosy.*

Habits of the people.

The census of Kumaun has been taken on three occasions within the last twenty years—in 1852, 1864, and in 1872. The population on the last occasion was found to be 406,042, and showed an increase of 46,000 during the

Census Returns.

* The "Report on the Census of British Burma" which, as already mentioned, reached us whilst this Report was in "proof," contains the following remarks regarding the improbability of the dirty habits of the people being, in the case of the Burmese, a predisposing cause of leprosy :—" This high ratio in British Burma is deserving of attention. With reference to the conditions under which it has been observed chiefly to prevail in other countries, it may be noted that the Burmese are neither a dirty nor an under-fed people, although it has been stated that they are addicted to injudicious forms of diet. How far the consumption of unwholesome wild vegetables and fish in a partially salted, half-putrescent state, is responsible for the presence of leprosy, it is beyond the scope of this summary to enquire."

The preparation of fish referred to is the well-known 'Ngapé,' which Colonel Yule thus describes :

"The paste of mashed and pickled fish, resembling very rank shrimp-paste, which is the favourite condiment of the Indo-Chinese races. It is the *Balachong* of the Malays, and the *Kapee* of Siam. Putrescent fish, in some shape or other, is a characteristic article of diet among all these races, from the mountains of Sylhet to the isles of the Archipelago. To the Chinese also, Sir John Bowring observes, fish is the more acceptable when it has a strong fragrance and flavour to give more gusto to the rice." With regard to the extent of its consumption in Burma, Colonel Yule mentions in another passage that during the year, from 1st November 1854 to 1st November 1855, 13,500 tons of *Ngapé* passed through the custom house at Thayetmyo as export from British to Independent Burma.—Yule's *Mission to the Court of Ava.*

In connection with this subject, compare the foregoing with the remarks regarding leprosy in Sicily in the foot-note at page 69.

twenty years following the first census. This population is equal to about one-third of that of North and South Wales together, and yields a mean of 58 persons to the square mile.

TABLE 4.—*Population of the District of Kumaun.*

CENSUS RETURNS FOR		
1852.	1864.	1872.
360,011	394,922	406,042

During our stay at Almora, General Ramsay very kindly placed these returns at our disposal, and appointed a clerk to transcribe the data regarding the number of lepers from the original census papers which were written in the vernacular.

Source of our statistical information.

These were arranged under the immediate supervision of the Officiating Junior Assistant Commissioner, Mr. G. H. Batten, to whom we are greatly indebted for the care with which he sifted the statistical records for us.

The country is divided into 19 sub-districts or *parganas,* each of which may be said to correspond to a county in England; and each of these parganas again is sub-divided into *pattis,* which may be described as parishes. Each patti has one of its leading men told off who is the recognised channel of communication between the inhabitants of the villages within its boundaries and the Civil authorities. It is through these officials that the population has been estimated.

The terms "pargana" and "patti."

We found that there was no absolute uniformity in the data supplied from the different pattis. In some of the returns no mention is made of the presence or absence of lepers in the particular district, whereas in other returns the halt, the blind, and the lepers are returned under one heading. And further, it is probable that, in the majority of instances, the cutaneous affection com-

Notwithstanding sources of error in the statistics,

monly spoken of by the people as "white leprosy"—*Leuco-derma*—has also been entered in the same column. These remarks apply to all three censuses. Moreover, not unfrequently lepers have been returned as residing in certain districts when the first census was taken, and similar entries are to be found in the last census, but all mention of them in the intervening census is omitted. Notwithstanding these drawbacks, however, the information regarding the distribution of leprosy approximates to the truth with an accuracy sufficient for all practical purposes. These statistics, moreover, have probably had the advantage of closer scrutiny than any other series embracing a like area in India, as not only has the marked prevalence of the disease in the district drawn the attention of the officials generally to the matter in a special manner, but the Commissioner has for more than thirty years personally taken the warmest interest in the subject, as may be inferred from his having founded an asylum at Almora to provide shelter for such of the lepers as were homeless, and in various other ways provided for the well-being of the poor creatures all over the country who, though leprous, were not actually wandering outcasts.

It may therefore, we think, be assumed that the data upon which these statistical observations are based are of more than average accuracy, and may be taken as fairly representing the general distribution of the disease in this part of the country, as well as sufficiently precise to afford evidence whether it be on the increase or on the decline among these hills.

it is probable that they are of more than average accuracy.

According to the first census that was taken of the district, there were 1,075 lepers, or very nearly equal to a ratio of 3 per thousand, the exact fraction being 2·98. Twelve years later the actual number of lepers returned was somewhat larger, being 1,128, but the proportion to the total population slightly diminished, *viz.*, 2·85 per mille, instead of 2·98. The returns which were received eight years later, however, showed a marked decrease both in the total numbers returned, 789, and in the proportion of lepers to the rest of the people, which, according to the census of 1872* (see page 22), was not quite 2 per 1,000, though very nearly so.

The three censuses analysed.

---

* These figures differ slightly from those given in the Census Report of the North-West Provinces.

There is little doubt, however, that these figures under-state rather than over-state the actual prevalence of the disease, for it is evident that for the most part only such of the lepers are entered as are actually more or less maimed by the disease. It is moreover notorious that the female lepers in a family are carefully kept out of sight, and consequently the returns regarding them are necessarily most defective. This in a great measure is the reason why the returning officers have not been able to register (on an average of all three censuses) more than one female for about every seven male lepers, although the probability is, so far as we have been able to ascertain, that female lepers are in reality nearly as numerous as male lepers in Kumaun.

The returns probably under-state the number of lepers, especially in the case of women.

It is evident therefore, for several reasons, that the figures regarding the prevalence of leprosy in this locality, as well as in India generally, can only be looked upon as approximately correct, and perhaps it will be nearer the truth were we to take the average number of lepers to the average total population in the three censuses. This average we find to be very nearly 1,000 lepers for the Kumaun District (not including Garhwal), or at the rate of 2·5 per mille of the average population during the last twenty-five years. These statistical details are brought together in the accompanying table.

Estimated number of lepers in the Kumaun District.

TABLE 5.—*Giving the Number of Lepers, and their Proportion to the Population, as ascertained from three Census Returns, together with the Mean of the three Returns.*

KUMAUN DISTRICT CENSUS RETURNS.

	1862.					1864.					1872.*					MEAN OF THE THREE RETURNS.				
	Total Population.	Lepers. Men.	Women.	Total.	Lepers per mille of Population.	Total Population.	Lepers. Men.	Women.	Total.	Lepers per mille of Population.	Total Population.	Lepers. Men.	Women.	Total.	Lepers per mille of Population.	Average total Population.	Average number of Lepers. Men.	Women.	Total.	Average number of Lepers per mille of Population.
	380,011	864	211	1,075	2·95	394,922	947	181	1,128	2·85	406,042	714	75	789	1·94	386,991	841·6	155·7	997·3	2·57

* These figures differ slightly from those given in the Census Report of the North-West Provinces.

2.—Is Leprosy exceptionally prevalent in Kumaun?

Assuming, therefore, that on an average 25 out of every 10,000 persons in the district are lepers, or taking the actual figures of the estimate, 1 leper to every 388 individuals, does this indicate that Kumaun is exceptionally unfortunate in this respect? We have already commented on the distribution of the malady over India generally in the opening chapter, and have found that it was only in comparatively a very few parts of the empire that the disease attained to the magnitude implied by a ratio of two per thousand; and when the entire divisions were taken, it was found that only in the division of Kumaun was this ratio exceeded. There are, however, a few *districts* in India in which the proportion is larger, especially some of the Districts (notably Beerbhoom) which go to form the Burdwan Division in Lower Bengal—a division in Bengal which alone contains nearly as many lepers as the whole of the Bombay Presidency,* so that Kumaun has the unenviable privilege of occupying a place at least in the front rank among the leprosy affected districts of British India.

The prevalence of Leprosy in Kumaun, compared with that of other districts.

With regard to the prevalence of leprosy in other countries, even the very complete Leprosy Report of the Royal College of Physicians published in 1867 contains but very few statistics, and so it is with other documents which we have examined: the writers, owing to paucity of information, have been compelled to restrict themselves "to general impressions." As is well known, the disease is in the present century less prevalent on the continent of Europe than on the other continents; nevertheless it is still endemic in many parts of Southern Europe,† and in some of the islands in the Mediterranean.

Leprosy in Europe and other countries.

---

* As an example of the want of definite information regarding these matters, the following remarks from a published official letter of comparatively recent date referring to the Collectorate (Division) of Ratnagherry in Bombay, may be cited:—" I cannot tell what the number of lepers may be in other collectorates, * * * but if the statements of a report I lately read be reliable, the whole Province of Bengal does not contain so many of this class of unfortunates as this single district." According to the Bombay Census Returns, Ratnagherry contains 1,287 lepers,—two per mille of population,—and the Province of Lower Bengal alone 28,403.

The Lepers of Ratnagherry.

† There are at the present time four most characteristic cases of leprosy in the wards of the Presidency General Hospital under Dr. Coull Mackenzie who have come from Greece for the express purpose of submitting themselves to medical treatment in Calcutta.

With regard to Sicily, for example, we have very recent information,* and the figures which have been published are of

Leprosy in Sicily.

interest in connection with the relation of leprosy to the sea-coast. It has been seen that in Madras the disease is more prevalent along the coast than in the interior; the reverse, however, holds good for Sicily, for whereas the returns gave 2 lepers to every 9,000 persons living along the coast, there were 5 persons to a similar number in the interior. Many parts of India may be cited as testifying to a similar condition.

Leprosy is also endemic to a serious extent in one at least of the countries of Northern Europe, *viz.*, Norway. Fortu-

Leprosy in Norway.

nately we have a mass of information regarding the disease as found in that country also, of the greatest value, thanks to the labours of the numerous Norwegian physicians who have investigated the subject, and to others not belonging to that country—notably Virchow, Vandyke Carter, and Neumann. In some respects comparisons may be instituted between Norway and Kumaun notwithstanding the difference in their position geographically, and the fact that the former is bounded on one side by the ocean; for, as Bishop Heber repeatedly observes in his "Journal,"† there are many physical features common to both; but these need not be specified on the present occasion. Norway contains about double the number of lepers that Kumaun does, but the population also of the former is more than three times that of the latter, so that the leprous population of Norway (12 per 10,000) is, in proportion, considerably lower than that of Kumaun.

With regard to the question whether leprosy is or is not on the increase in the district under consideration, it will be

Is Leprosy on the increase in Kumaun?

seen that the number of lepers actually registered in the last census was smaller than was registered in 1864. However, on looking carefully over

* Profeta "Sulla Lepra in Sicilia," September 1875. Vide "*Jahresbericht über die gesammten Medicin*" (Virchow und Hirsch), für 1875; Band I. Seite 431.

† In one of these passages the Bishop remarks: "The country as we advanced became exceedingly beautiful and romantic. It reminded me most of Norway, but had the advantage of round-topped trees instead of the unwearied spear-like outline of the pine. It would have been like some parts of Wales had not the hills and precipices been much higher, and the valleys, or rather dells, narrower and more savage. We could seldom, from the range on which the road ran, see to the bottom of any of them, and only heard the roar and rush of the river which we had left, and which the torrents which foamed across our path were hastening to join."—*Bishop Heber's Indian Journal*, Vol. 1: 1843.

and comparing the various entries in the detailed census
returns for the several years, and taking into consideration
the general impression entertained by so many of the officials
in the district whom we consulted, and especially of such
of the officers whose duties have constantly taken them for
several years past into immediate contact with the population
of even the remotest villages, we are of opinion that the
number of lepers has not diminished to the extent which the
last census returns imply, so that probably the earlier censuses were more exact than the last regarding this matter.
The following fact appears to support this view :—

A reference to Table 5 on page 22 will show that in
the census of 1852 the number of male to female lepers
was nearly as 4 to 1, whereas in the last census the number
of male was almost ten times that of the female lepers—a
proportion which seems to be farther from the truth than
that yielded by the earlier census.

On a future occasion we hope to be able to submit more
precise data regarding this matter; at present our impression
is, that although leprosy is probably decreasing in the district,
the decrease is not quite to the extent suggested by the
figures.

3.—*The Geographical Distribution of Leprosy in Kumaun.*

With the view of carrying out to the fullest extent practicable the suggestion of the
Army Sanitary Commission already referred to, that not only
the numerical data but the precise localities where leprosy
prevails should be ascertained, we have kept not only the records of each pargana (= county?) distinct for itself for the
different years, but also the data regarding each patti
(= parish?), and every town and village within its limits.
The information thus collected was graphically represented
on charts of the district so as to ascertain whether a more
clear conception of the distribution of the malady could
be obtained by this means than was obtainable by a study
of the figures alone. It was our intention originally to have
reproduced the greater portion of these charts, but we found
that they all told pretty much the same story, and we have
therefore decided on reproducing merely the chart which
illustrates the distribution of the disease as deduced from the
average ratios of the three censuses. We have, however,
reproduced a condensed tabular statement showing the prevalence of the disease in the various parganas for all the

periods mentioned, as well as the series of figures upon which the scale-shading of the map is based, which will be found in the fourth column of figures in the table.

TABLE 6.—*Showing the distribution of Leprosy in each Pargana in Kumaun according to the Census of 1852, 1864, and 1872, together with the Mean of the Three Returns, arranged in order of severity in each case.*

	1852 Census.				1864 Census.				1872 Census.				Mean of the Three Returns.		
Order of severity.	Pargana.	Total Lepers.	Lepers per mille of population.	Order of severity.	Pargana.	Total Lepers.	Lepers per mille of population.	Order of severity.	Pargana.	Total Lepers.	Lepers per mille of population.	Order of severity.	Pargana.	Average total number of Lepers.	Average number of Lepers per mille of population.
1	Sor ...	109	5·94	1	Chaugarkha	178	6·07	1	Chaugarkha	99	3·77	1	Chaugarkha	132	4·83
2	Chaugarkha	121	4·74	2	Sor ...	96	5·05	2	Káli Kumaun.	168	3·52	2	Sor ...	98	4·82
3	Sirá ...	19	4·20	3	Gangoli ...	74	3·74	3	Sor	76	3·47	3	Gangoli ...	64	3·37
4	Ramgarh ...	18	3·70	4	Bárahmandal.	209	3·31	4	Gangoli ...	62	3·10	4	Káli Kumaun.	139	3·04
5	Bárahmandal.	203	3·49	5	Phaldákot...	52	3·19	5	Sirá ...	23	2·66	5	Sirá ...	20	3·00
6	Gangoli ...	56	3·29	6	Dánpur ...	62	3·01	6	Askot ...	15	2·44	6	Askot ...	15	2·79
7	Askot ...	15	3·11	7	Askot ...	17	2·88	7	Dánpur ...	51	2·02	7	Bárahmandal.	174	2·71
8	Káli Kumaun.	188	3·05	8	Kotauli } 9 Mahryúri }	32	2·66	8	Kota ...	1	1·95	8	Dánpur ...	54	2·59
9	Dánpur ...	49	2·97	10	Sirá ...	21	2·60	9	Bárahmandal.	110	1·67	9	Phaldákot...	40	2·49
10	Phaldákot...	40	2·77	11	Páli ...	246	2·59	10	Phaldákot	28	1·54	10	Páli ...	19	2·10
11 Kotauli } 12 Mahryúri }		30	2·67	12	Káli Kumaun.	111	2·51	11	Páli ...	123	1·31	11 Kotauli } 12 Mahryúri }		22	1·64
13	Páli ...	211	2·42	13	Kotá ...	9	1·95	12	Dhyánirau	16	0·91	13	Chhakháta	9	1·20
14	Chhakháta	13	1·79	14	Ramgarh ...	6	1·16	13	Chhakháta	5	0·65	14	Kota ...	5	1·25
15	Dhaniyakot	17	1·48	15	Dármá ...	8	0·62	14 Kotauli } 15 Mahryúri }		6	0·49	15	Dhyánirau...	19	1·10
16	Dhyánirau	22	1·23	16	Johár ...	6	0·60	16	Johár ...	4	0·38	16	Ramgarh...	5	1·00
17	Koti ...	5	1·06	17	Dhaniyakot	6	0·47	17	Ramgarh ...	1	0·19	17	Dhaniyakot	8	0·70
18	Johár ...	9	0·96	18	Chhakháta	?	?	18	Dhaniyakot	2	0·17	18	Johár ...	6	0·64
19	Dárma ...	?	?	19	Dhyánirau	?	?	19	Dármá ...	?	?	19	Dármá ...	3	0·62

A glance at the figures and at the map is sufficient to arrest attention at once to the fact that leprosy prevails to a far greater extent along the eastern side of the district than along the western. This is not

The map shows that the disease prevails along the eastern side.

MAP ILLUSTRATING THE **DISTRIBUTION** o

[Shaded according to the Proportionate Prevalenc

LEPERS PER 1,000 OF

PARGANAHS.		
1 Sor	} 4 to 5 per 1,000	
2 Chaugarkha		
3 Gangoli	} 3 to 4 per 1,000	
4 Kálikumaun		
5 Sirá		
6 Askot		
7 Bárahmandal		
8 Dánpur	} 2 to 3 per 1,000	
9 Phaldákot		
10 Pali		

p
tl
in

T

=

Order of severity.

1
2
3
4
5
6
7
8
9
10
11
12
13
14

15

16
17
18
19

1

1

only the story which the figures of any particular census convey, nor yet of the average of all three censuses, but of each of them independently. As a rule, also, the most populous districts, and probably the most well-to-do, are those containing the largest ratio of lepers.

We have found it impracticable to represent graphically any information regarding the comparative prevalence of the disease in the valleys and on the hills on the present occasion. This is a question which it will be more convenient to discuss after the investigation of the localities themselves has been made. Indeed, the utmost that we can attempt at present on this point is to indicate generally the parts of the district where the malady is most prevalent.

Notwithstanding the fact that the same parganas (or counties) persistently maintain a larger ratio of such persons, a study of the figures of these

The leprous population a shifting one.

censuses tends to indicate that the leprous population is a shifting one so far as the particular towns and villages which they frequent is concerned ; for the papers before us show that out of an average of 574 communities which contained lepers, taking all three censuses, only 35 of all these communities are found entered as containing lepers in all three returns. This peculiarity can, we think, hardly be fully accounted for by referring it to registration-errors. We have endeavoured to analyse these returns still further in order to elucidate this matter, and find that although in some places, such as shrines and the like, there is a decided tendency to the aggregation of a number of lepers, nevertheless the more general distribution appears to be pretty equal amongst the population. For example, out of the above given average of 574 communities in Kumaun associated with lepers, there were only 63 communities, taking the average of the three censuses, that contained 4 lepers, or a percentage of 4 or more. At present these facts are merely put on record because they deserve attention, but any detailed remarks which a study of them suggests will be more profitably made when the local inquiries have been completed.

4.—What are the main features in connection with the localities in which it is most prevalent ?

Having seen that three out of the four leading questions which we set ourselves at starting may be replied to pretty

The fourth query.

conclusively from a study of the statistics alone,—*viz.* (*1st*), to what extent are the inhabitants of the district of Kumaun affected with leprosy ? (*2ndly*), whether this district is affected in an exceptionally severe manner; and (*3rdly*) whether the disease is more prevalent in any particular portion of it: the fourth question suggests itself naturally out of the reply to the third,—namely, To what may the ascertained prevalence of the disease along the eastern side be attributed?

Seeing that we purpose going over these particular portions of the district, it will be best to defer all reference to the physical features of the locality which records might supply until we shall have been able to obtain information for ourselves regarding them: but one feature we cannot avoid directing attention to even thus early in the course of the inquiry; and that is the fact that the portions of the district which are specially affected are directed towards the Nepal frontier.

Leprosy in Nepal.

Although our exact knowledge of the distribution of disease in Nepal is exceedingly meagre, on account of the hindrance offered by the Nepal authorities to the exploration of the country by Europeans, still it is well known that leprosy does prevail to a large extent in that territory. The neighbouring Nepalese and the Kumaunese are for the most part derived from the same stock; the hills and valleys which they inhabit are alike, and so are their habits; and it is highly probable that the customs which prevailed for many centuries in Kumaun during the reigns of the local rajahs until 1790, and subsequently under the rule of the Goorkhas, until they in their turn were ejected by the British in 1815, continue unmodified, or modified to a very trifling extent only, in these portions of Nepal at the present day. Now, with regard to the custom of the country in connection with leprosy, we have very trustworthy information that when a person became a confirmed leper he somehow disappeared, and there were no questions asked. They were supposed to have buried themselves. This state of affairs of course disappeared with the accession of British rule, but as British authority does not extend beyond the River Káli, it seems not improbable that the Nepalese lepers, foreseeing a possible contingency, cross this river, and thus avail themselves of the protection of a more humane government. It appears to us, therefore, not to be a circumstance to create surprise to find that the Nepal side of our territory should be thus exceptionally frequented by lepers.

This deduction is strongly supported by the somewhat remarkable circumstance that, notwithstanding the distance
between Almora and the Nepalese frontier, one-fifth of all
the lepers who have obtained shelter at the asylum during
the last thirty years came from Nepal.

B.—Observations conducted at the Almora Leper Asylum.

HAVING in the previous section discussed some of the general questions relating to the existence and prevalence of leprosy in Kumaun, we now proceed to give an account of the information derived from an examination of the present inmates and past history of the Leper Asylum at Almora.

The Asylum has now been in existence for upwards of 30 years, and there can be no question as to the benefit which Sir Henry Ramsay has conferred on the people of Kumaun in establishing and supporting the institution. Lepers, although in some cases kindly treated by their friends, are no doubt in very many exposed to great ill-usage. The aversion with which they are regarded, and the disgrace attaching to the occurrence of the disease in a family, are inducements to make outcasts of them, and the temptation to do so is increased by interested motives, as, by turning them adrift, their relatives are enabled to appropriate to their own use the share of the family property belonging to the sick. Under these circumstances an asylum, utterly apart from benefits due to medical treatment, is a great blessing to the unhappy lepers, affording them a shelter in which they may live in comparative comfort, in place of wandering at large over the country as beggars. In striking proof of this is the rarity with which leprous beggars, in spite of the prevalence of the disease, are to be encountered in the neighbourhood of Almora, as well as the contented and even cheerful spirit displayed by the vast majority of the inmates of the Asylum, which cannot fail to be remarked by all who are aware of the miserable and depressed condition of similar cases occurring in places where no proper accommodation is provided for them.

(marginal note: The period during which the Leper Asylum at Almora has been in existence, and the benefits conferred on the district by its institution.)

We are under great obligation to the Honorary Superintendent of the Asylum, the Reverend J. H. Budden, for the readiness with which he aided us in ascertaining the fullest particulars regarding the institution and its inmates, as also to all the officers who were in any way connected with the Asylum.

1.—*Summary of the Statistical Records of the Asylum.*

The following tables show the principal facts in the history of the Asylum, relative to admissions, number of inmates, mortality, &c., obtainable from the registers kept in the institution :

TABLE 7.—*Number of Male Lepers admitted into the Leper Asylum at Almora, with the numbers of those who have died, of those who have left the Asylum, and of those remaining in it.*

Years.	Total male lepers admitted.	Years in which deaths occurred.											Total deaths.	Left the Asylum.	Remaining in the Asylum.
		1866.	1867.	1868.	1869.	1870.	1871.	1872.	1873.	1874.	1875.	1876.			
Previous to 1866	13	...	...	...	...	...	...	...	1	2	1	...	4	3	6
1866	2	...	...	...	...	...	...	1	...	...	...	...	1	...	1
1867	3	...	...	...	.	...	...	...	1	2	...	...	3	...	..
1868	10	...	...	...	...	...	1	1	2	1	...	...	5	3	2
1869	7	...	...	...	...	...	...	1	1	...	...	...	2	...	5
1870	11	...	...	...	...	...	...	2	3	...	1	1	7	1	3
1871	14	...	...	...	...	...	...	2	...	4	...	...	6	6	2
1872	12	...	...	...	...	...	...	1	2	1	...	...	4	4	4
1873	16	...	...	...	...	...	...	...	6	2	...	...	8	2	6
1874	17	...	...	...	...	...	...	...	...	4	...	...	4	7	6
1875	11	...	...	...	...	...	...	...	...	...	2	1	3	1	7
1876	11	...	...	...	...	...	...	...	...	...	...	1	1	2	8
TOTAL	127	...	...	...	...	...	...	7	16	17	5	3	48	29	50

TABLE 8.—*Number of Female Lepers admitted into the Asylum at Almora, with the numbers of those who have died, of those who have left the Asylum, and of those remaining in it.*

YEARS.	Total female lepers admitted.	YEARS IN WHICH FEMALE LEPERS DIED.												Left the Asylum.	Number remaining.
		1866.	1867.	1868.	1869.	1870.	1871.	1872.	1873.	1874.	1875.	1876.	Total deaths.		
Previous to } 1866	23	...	...	...	...	...	...	1	4	1	4	...	10	2	11
1866	2	...	...	...	...	...	...	...	...	...	1	...	1	...	1
1867	3	...	...	...	...	...	...	...	...	1	2	...	3	...	...
1868	3	...	...	...	...	...	...	1	...	...	1	...	2	...	1
1869	2	...	...	...	...	...	...	...	...	...	...	...	...	...	2
1870	5	...	...	...	...	...	...	...	...	...	...	...	...	1	4
1871	9	...	...	...	...	...	...	...	...	1	2	...	3	1	5
1872	7	...	...	...	...	...	...	2	1	...	...	...	3	3	1
1873	8	...	...	...	...	...	...	...	1	1	...	...	2	4	2
1874	8	...	...	...	...	...	...	...	...	3	...	...	3	2	3
1875	8	...	...	...	...	...	...	...	...	...	...	1	1	1	6
1876	6	...	...	...	...	...	...	...	...	...	...	...	...	...	6
TOTAL ...	84	...	...	...	...	...	...	4	6	7	10	1	28	14	42

During the entire period in which the Asylum has been in existence, 211 patients—127 males and 84 females—have been received into it up to the end of June 1876. Since 1866, from which date alone accurate registration has been conducted, the numbers present in the Asylum in any year have, on an average, amounted to 97·2, ranging from 106 in 1869 to 85 in the commencement of the current year. The numbers annually admitted have varied from 4 in 1866 to 25 in 1874. Previous to 1866, 13 males and 23 females were admitted. Since that time the number of males admitted has, almost every year, largely exceeded that of females—a fact which is no doubt greatly due, as has been already pointed out in regard to the census returns, to a

Summary of the history of Asylum; number of inmates, deaths, &c.

greater tendency to conceal the occurrence of the disease when occurring in females. Of the total of 211 cases admitted, 43 have left the Asylum at various dates and 76 have died. As the patients are under no restraint, the comparatively small number leaving speaks well for the comfort enjoyed by the inmates.

The deaths since 1866 have varied from 24 in 1874 to 11 in 1872. No deaths have been recorded as having occurred between 1866 and 1872, but 36 per cent. of the total cases admitted, or 45·2 per cent. of the admissions after deducting those leaving the Asylum, have died since 1872. The causes of death in the various years cannot now be determined, as, until quite recently, there was no medical establishment connected with the institution. This is to be regretted, as the fluctuations in the number of deaths is very considerable. Such an absence of information fortunately cannot occur again, as the Asylum is now under the supervision of a medical officer, and has a resident native doctor attached permanently to it. Of the 36 lepers admitted into the Asylum previous to 1866, 14, or 38·8 per cent., are dead; the rest, with the exception of 5, are now in the Asylum. Of the 175 cases admitted since 1866, 62, or 35·4 per cent., have died, 38 have left the Asylum, and 75 remain. That the percentage of deaths should be so nearly equal in the two cases is no doubt owing to the fact that the majority of deaths occur among recent admissions, and are probably due to the tuberculated form of leprosy, which is known to run a more rapid course than the anæsthetic form. The number of inmates of the Asylum during our visit was 80, excluding a few spurious or doubtful cases.

The Mortuary Returns of the Asylum.

All the recognised forms of true leprosy are represented among the inmates, although in very unequal proportion, there being 49 cases in which anæsthetic phenomena form the prominent symptoms, 12 in which the tubercular element prevails, 4 in which eruption is very conspicuous, and 15 in which tuberculated and anæsthetic phenomena are so closely and equally associated that they may with propriety be regarded as cases of the "mixed" variety of leprosy.* This division of the cases is,

All forms and stages of leprosy represented among the inmates.

---

* These figures do not give a total corresponding with that derived from the tables of admissions, due to the fact that a few doubtful cases are inmates of the Asylum.

however, to be regarded as a relative one only, founded on predominance of symptoms. The cases classed as "anæsthetic" were invariably, or almost invariably, comparatively pure cases of this form; but in advanced cases of tuberculated leprosy, the phenomena are very rarely, if ever, dissociated from more or less pronounced symptoms of anæsthesia, so that they might generally be included under the heading of mixed cases. Still the one condition was so much more strongly marked than the other, that it appeared warrantable and conducive to clearness to retain them under a distinct heading. The same holds in regard to those classed as "eruptive," the very small proportion of which cases is noteworthy, and is probably, in part at all events, to be ascribed to the fact that patients do not generally present themselves for admission until the disease has lasted for some time, and until, in consequence, eruptive symptoms have disappeared, or have been obscured by the development of anæsthetic or tuberculated phenomena. This is the more probable as, in the vast majority of cases, the patients suffering from advanced tubercular or anæsthetic symptoms described their disease as having commenced with the occurrence of an eruption.

Whilst at Almora we endeavoured to select typical examples of the two leading forms of *The accompanying illustrations.* leprosy for the purpose of illustrating their more prominent features. Several such cases were photographed, but we have thought that three would be sufficient for our present purpose. Reproductions of these are appended to the present report.

Speaking generally, the plates may serve as illustrations both of the anæsthetic and tuberculated forms of the disease. The *Plates I and II.* eruption presents a prominent feature in the case which we selected of the former (Plate I), especially on the dorsal surface of the trunk; but numerous little nodular elevations may also be observed when the photograph of the chest of the same individual is closely examined (Plate II). It will also be remarked that almost complete absorption of the fingers has taken place.

In the figures of the third plate the tuberculated feature is the leading characteristic. *Plate III, Figures 1 and 2.* Figure 1 (Plate III) represents an almost typical instance of the *Leontiasis* of the Ancients. The lips are thickened; the skin of the forehead is thrown

Plate 1.

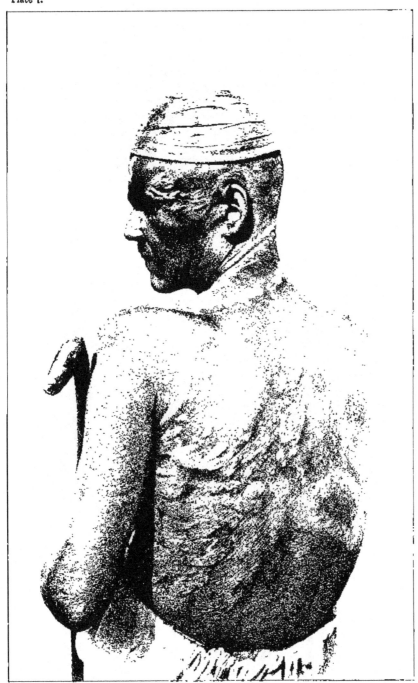

From a Photograph.

ANÆSTHETIC FORM OF LEPROSY—The Eruption.

Plate II.

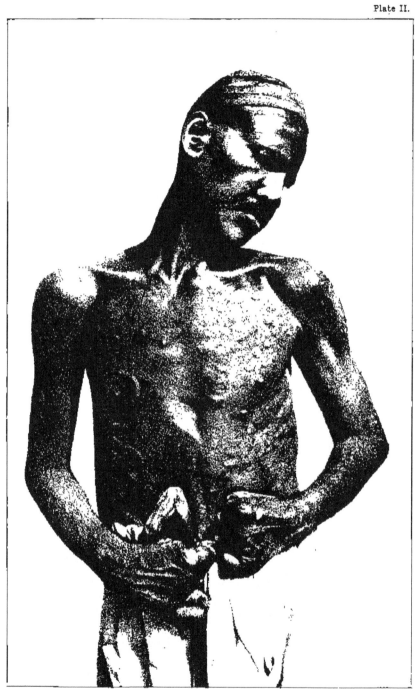

From a Photograph.

ANÆSTHETIC FORM OF LEPROSY—Destruction of Fingers.

[The same patient as in Plate I.]

into nodular folds separated by deep furrows; the eyebrows and lobes of the ears are enormously thickened, as are also the *Alæ. Nasi :* the latter are seen to have acquired a trefoil-like aspect. In Figure 2 (Plate III) the thickening of the lips and ears, and the sinking of the *septum nasi,* owing to disease of the mucous membrane and cartilages of the nose, are conspicuous. In addition there is an angry lupus-looking ulcer of the cheek which had produced even more distortion of the features than is suggested by the plate. These cases will be subsequently referred to when detailing the clinical observations.

In proceeding to details, we shall first give an account of the facts ascertained in reference to each class of cases separately, and shall then proceed to the consideration of those questions common to the disease generally.

2.—*Analysis of cases in the Asylum affected with Anæsthetic Leprosy.*

This is, as has been shown above, much the commonest form of the disease among the inmates of the Asylum.

Anæsthetic leprosy the common-est form in the Asylum.

The distribution and extent of the anæsthesia present varied extremely in different cases. Taking the 49 cases, the general distribution of the anæs-thesia is shown in the following statement :—

TABLE 9.—*Showing the Distribution of Anæsthesia in 49 Lepers.*

Cases	ANÆSTHESIA OF						
	HEAD AND NECK.				Upper Extremities.	Lower Extremities.	Trunk.
	Face.	Ears.	Scalp.	Neck.			
49	36	28	12	6	48	49	21

In this statement we find that in 36 cases there was more or less complete anæsthesia of the face, that in 28 the ears, in 12 the scalp, in 6 the neck, in 48 the upper, in all the lower extremities, and in 21 the trunk, were affected. In 2 cases the ears were affected without

Distribution of anæsthesia over the body.

there being any anæsthesia of the face, so that the cases in which the head and neck were affected amounted as a total to 38. Taking the regions of the entire body in order of number of cases, we find the lower extremities occupying the first place, followed successively by the upper extremities, the head and neck, and the trunk, the latter being only a little more than half as frequently affected as the face.

Proceeding to a more detailed account of the distribution of the anæsthesia, we shall take up its several localities in the order of the table.

1. The face.—In 20 cases the anæsthesia was complete over the entire face. In those

Facts regarding anæsthesia of the face.

cases in which it was partial only, the precise distribution varied; in one case it was confined to the malar prominences, in another to the right malar prominence and the centre of the forehead, while in a third there was complete anæsthesia of one side of the face, the other remaining unaffected. The chin alone escaped in three cases, along with the upper lip in another, and with the upper lip and the angles of the lower jaw in a third. In two cases the forehead alone, in one the forehead and the upper lip, and in one the temporal regions alone escaped. In four cases the precise distribution was not determined.

2. The ears.—In 18 cases these were entirely anæsthetic. In one there was complete anæs-

The ears. Tendency of the interior surfaces and tragi to retain sensation.

thesia of the left ear only; in five sensibility was impaired, although not absent; in two the tragi and interior surface of the ears escaped; in one the interior of both ears with the tragus of the right, and in another the interior of the right ear alone escaped.

3. The scalp.—In eight cases anæsthesia was complete over the entire forehead. In one

Distribution of anæsthesia on the forehead.

it extended from the forehead half-way to the occiput; in one it was present on the left side only, and in one a certain amount of sensibility was retained throughout. In one case the precise distribution was not determined.

4. The neck.—Anæsthesia of the neck when present was in all cases complete over the

Rarity of anæsthesia of the neck.

entire region, and its occurrence was always associated with very widely diffused and extreme anæsthesia of the body generally.

5. *The upper extremities.*—In 20 cases the entire upper extremities from the shoulders downwards were completely anæsthetic. In 13 cases anæsthesia was complete from the elbows, in two complete from the elbows save over the hollow in front of the joint. In one case it was confined to the extensor surfaces from a little above the elbows, and in another was complete from the elbows on the extensor and only partial on the flexor surfaces. In one case the entire upper extremities, save the ball and inner margin of the left thumb, were affected; in one the entire extensor surfaces with the flexor surfaces from a little above the elbows. In one case anæsthesia was not present save over the upper third of the inner surfaces of the arms. In one case it was complete from the mid-forearms; in one it was complete from the elbow downwards on the right side, but on the other was confined to the hand; in one it was present from the elbow downwards on the right side for the entire surface, on the left for the extensor surface only. In one case the left extremity was entirely anæsthetic, whilst the upper portion of the right arm retained sensation. In one the hands alone were affected, in one the extensor surfaces alone from a little above the elbow. In one the extensor surfaces throughout and the entire hands, save the tips of the fore and ring fingers and the ball of the right thumb, were anæsthetic ; in another the anæsthesia was complete, save over the upper third of the inner surfaces of the arms. In no cases were the arms affected without the forearms; in one there was no anæsthesia present ; in one only it was confined to the hands, and in five there was evidence of a greater liability to disease of the extensor as compared with the flexor surfaces.

Distribution of anæsthesia over the upper extremities.

6. *The lower extremities.*—In 18 of the 49 cases the entire extremities were affected; in 15 complete anæsthesia was present from the knees downwards; in one the condition was similar, save that the areas corresponding with the lower half of the popliteal spaces were sensitive. In four cases complete anæsthesia was present from the mid-thigh; in one from mid-thigh anteriorly, and over the entire posterior surface, save the popliteal areas. In three cases there was complete anæsthesia from the knees with diminished sensibility of the thighs; in two the anæsthesia was universal, save over the upper third of the inner

Anæsthesia of the lower extremities present in all of the cases.

surface of the thighs; in one it was complete over the entire surface externally and posteriorly, and from the ankles only on the inner surface. In one case the popliteal area of the right side alone escaped. In one anæsthesia was present from the upper third of the legs; in one from the ankles, and in one confined to the feet.

7. *The trunk.*—In five cases the entire surface of the trunk was completely anæsthetic, and in another the patient affirm-

Anæsthesia of the trunk.

ed this to be the case, although at the same time distinct twitching of the surface followed irritation. In four cases sensibility, although much diminished, was not absent, and in one of these the posterior was less affected than the anterior surface. In one there was partial anæsthesia passing into total absence of sensation over the gluteal regions; in one there was complete anæsthesia anteriorily, and in another complete anæsthesia posteriorily. In one anæsthesia was confined to the shoulders; in four to the gluteal regions; in one to the left gluteal region; in one to the loins; and in another to a patch behind the spleen.

The general results of this analysis of cases illustrate the well-known tendency to peri-

Peripheral localisation of anæsthesia and its distribution according to nervous areas.

pheral over central localisation of the affection, and also clearly demonstrate the distribution of anæsthesia according to nervous areas. One of the most interesting points noted is that in reference to the ears, apparently indicating that the internal surfaces and the tragi are less liable to suffer than the rest of the ears, implying a corresponding comparative exemption of the auriculo-temporal nerve as compared with the other nerves supplying the external ear. The distribution according to nervous areas is also illustrated by other phenomena—by the exemption of the upper lip and chin, by the sharp limitation of anæsthesia to the line of the lower jaw and to the gluteal regions on the trunk, by the greater liability of the extensor as compared with the flexor surfaces of the upper, and of the outer with the inner surfaces of the lower extremities.

Having thus discussed the phenomena of the diminution, or disappearance, of the

Other nervous symptoms present in anæsthetic cases.

sensibility of the external surface of the body, there yet remain one or two anæsthetic and other nervous symptoms to be noted in reference to the cases. The condition of the tongue and fauces in relation to common and special sensation was inquired into in numerous cases. As a rule, both touch and taste, according to the patient's account, remained intact, and only in very advanced cases was there any evidence of loss of either. In one case the tongue was anæsthetic to touch, but the sense of taste was retained, whilst in another the reverse condition was present.

In four cases only did the patients complain of any pain, Pain only present in four cases. in spite of the great prevalence of open ulcerating surfaces among them. In one the sites of pain were referred to the inner side of the right and outer side of the left calves, extending to the knee-joints, and a certain amount of prominence of the cutaneous nerves over corresponding areas could be detected. In another case pain was complained of along the inner sides of both calves, in a third the big toes were painful, and in another the pain was connected with ulcerations of the soles of the feet. In several other cases, although no general complaint of pain was made, the exposed surfaces of the phalanges of the fingers and toes were tender and painful when touched. That pain cannot be a common or troublesome accompaniment of leprosy among the inmates of the Almora Asylum is sufficiently evident from the happy and cheerful demeanour manifested by the majority of them.

Dimness of vision was complained of in one case. The Dimness of vision. eyes showed no external signs of disease, but as an opthalmoscopic examination could not be made it remains uncertain whether or not this were due to the existence of deposit on the retina. In one very advanced case the patient was blind, but this was due to opacity of the cornea.

In one or two cases there were obvious thickenings along the course of the cutaneous Condition of the skin; shrivelling of the surface, discolored patches, fissures, &c. nerves supplying anæsthetic areas. The skin in many instances showed no special indications of disease apart from ulcerations or the cicatricial traces of former ones. In 17 cases, however, there were more or less decided alterations in the skin over the surface of one or other portion of the body. The commoner forms of these were general shrivelling and puckering of the surface, which at the same time presented a peculiarly dry aspect; the occurrence of coarse folds of skin about the elbows and knees; the presence of fissures in the hands, and more especially in the soles of the feet, and the occurrence of discolored patches of various extent. The cause of the shrivelled and folded condition of the skin is no doubt to be ascribed in great part to partial atrophy and diminution in bulk of the subjacent muscles, and may in part also be due to affection of its intrinsic muscular elements. The cracking of the skin is a very common symptom, and is, as we shall see, frequently the first to warn the patient of the onset of disease. The patches of discoloration were sometimes of a whitish hue, and were then usually situated about the elbows, knees, hands, and feet. In three cases there were large irregular patches of light discoloration, probably the remains of leprous eruption, over the back and shoulders; and in one the same regions were occupied by similar patches of pinkish color. In one case the hands and feet were swollen and scaly, and in another a scaly eruption was present over the ankles. In two cases there was a very peculiar bluish cyanotic hue of the palms of the hands.

In one case there was marked enlargement of the inguinal glands. In 35 cases open ulcers were present, sometimes on both the hands and feet, very rarely on the hands alone, frequently on the feet alone. They were in many ascribed to burns or other injuries incurred, due to the anæsthetic condition of the affected surfaces, and this probably is the explanation of their more frequent occurrence on the feet. In most cases they were said to heal readily and easily, which, with the phenomena frequently attending their causation, points to the non-specific or essentially leprous nature of many of such ulcers, not being dependent on the breaking down of any deposit, but merely due to accidents or mal-nutrition induced by the effects of such deposit elsewhere. This is a point on which Virchow lays particular stress.* The inference is also borne out by the microscopic examination of the discharges from such ulcerating surfaces, for, in so far as we could ascertain from those cases in which we examined such materials, they contain no special cells or other morphological elements not common to any non-specific ulcerating surfaces.

Enlargement of the glands.

Ulcers; their character and causation.

---

* *Die Krankhaften Geschwülste.* Zweiter Band; Seite 529.

In only three cases was there an entire freedom from
ulceration or absorption of the

Loss of digits almost universal to
a greater or less degree.

digits of both hands and feet.
In all the rest one or other
condition was present in greater or less degree, sometimes
affecting the hands or even one hand only, whilst the feet
escaped, in others having a reversed distribution, but in
the vast majority affecting both upper and lower extremities
simultaneously. The degree to which the affection of the
digits was present varied greatly, ranging from mere cracks
and superficial ulceration of the tips of one or two fingers
or toes up to the total absence of the whole of all of
them, and in some cases even to partial disappearance of
one or more metacarpal bones (*vide* Plate II). In most
cases the mutilation appeared to have been caused by progressive ulceration or by necroses *en masse* of one or more
joints at a time, but in some the digits appeared rather
to have been removed by a process of interstitial absorption, as the nails, in a more or less entire condition, adhered
to the remnants of hands or feet which still persisted.

In many cases the remaining digits were strongly contracted, the contraction in some

Distortions due to contraction,
muscular atrophy, &c.

instances causing most curious
distortions, as in those where
there was permanent flexion of the proximal phalanges
with extension of the distal one of one or more fingers—a
condition present in several instances.

In advanced cases of long duration there was frequently,
in addition to distortion due to contraction, extreme muscular atrophy, the entire muscles of the ball of the thumb
and palms of the hands appearing to have disappeared,
leaving the bony framework covered by the skin alone.
This was especially remarkable in one or two old cases in
which the disease had lasted for many years unaccom-
panied by much distortion or destruction of the hands.

The voice was more or less altered and husky in seven
cases. In five of these the nose

Affection of the voice.

was sunken, and in several it
was difficult to determine whether the condition was not
due rather to syphilitic than to leprous disease. In two at
all events there could be little doubt in referring it to
syphilis; in one of these there was most offensive ozæna,
and in the other the depression of the nose was affirmed to
have preceded the leprous symptoms.

The blood of the patients was microscopically examined in 28 cases. In 17 of these it was to all appearance perfectly normal, in the remaining 11 it

The microscopical characters of the blood.

was characterised in five instances by a greater or less excess of normal white corpuscles and bioplastic fragments of small size, in three by such excess combined with a softened gelatinous condition of the red corpuscles causing them to adhere in irregular masses, and in three by the latter phenomenon alone. In two, specimens of blood could only be with difficulty obtained from the hands. One of these was a case in which the characters of the specimen were normal; the other, one in which the red corpuscles were softened. In both cases the difficulty seemed to arise from the presence of much condensation of the tissues at the site of puncture due to absorptive and cicatricial changes there. In most cases the blood was obtained with ease, and in some there was an excessive tendency to hæmorrhage on the slightest provocation.

These are the principal phenomena noted in regard to the condition of the subjects of anæsthetic leprosy in the Asylum, and it now remains to consider one or two more general points in their history.

Sex.—Of the 49 cases of the anæsthetic variety of the disease, 25 were males and 24 females, giving respectively a percentage of 54·3 and·70·5 on

Sex of the cases of anæsthetic leprosy.

the total male and female leprous population of the Asylum.*

Age.—The ages of the patients ranged from 17 to 63, the average of all being 40·9. In regard to this as well as in regard to the age of attack,

The age. Difficulty of obtaining correct information regarding it.

and consequently of the duration of disease, the data are avowedly imperfect and to be taken as only relatively correct, as the natives of India are habitually so ignorant of their actual age and so incorrect in their estimates of time, that no reliance can be placed on the accuracy of their statements on such subjects. Taking the figures as they are, the earliest date of attack is 8 years, and the latest 60. Of the forty-nine cases five are said to have commenced under 10 years of age, twelve between 10 and 20, twelve between 20 and 30,

---

* These percentages refer to the distinctly leprous inmates only.

thirteen between 30 and 40, three between 30 and 40, three between 50 and 60, and one at 60.

The average age of attack for the 49 cases is 26·18.

The average age of attack and the duration of disease. The duration of disease from the date of attack until the period of examination ranged from 1 to 40 years. That of sixteen was under 10 years, of fifteen between 10 and 20 years, of sixteen between 20 and 30, of one 32 years, and of one 40 years. In regard to the latter case, the disease appeared almost in abeyance, having apparently run its course, and left the patient suffering from the effects of former rather than from the existence of present disease. There could be no doubt as to the prolonged course of the disease in this instance, as the patient has been for 32 years an inmate of the Asylum. The average duration for the 49 cases was 15·22 years.

Existence of leprosy among relatives. The question of the existence of leprosy among the patients' relatives was carefully inquired into with the following results. In 18 of the 49 cases of the anæsthetic form of the affection, or 36·7 per cent., the patients allowed that they had, at the time of examination or formerly, leprous relatives. The nature of the relationship is shown in the following statement:—

TABLE 10.—*Cases of Anæsthetic Leprosy with leprous relatives.*

No.	NATURE OF RELATIONSHIP.			
	Parents.	Brothers or Sisters.	Children.	Other relatives.
1	Both ...	3 Brothers.		
2	,, ...			
3	,, ...			
4	Mother ...	1 Sister.		
5	,, ...	1 Brother ...	...	Mother's brother.
6	,, ...			
7	,, ...			
8	,, ...			
9	,, ...			
10	... ...	1 Brother.		
11	... ...	,,		
12	... ...	,,		
13	... ...	,,		
14	... ...	... ...	4 Sons.	
15	... ...	... ...	...	Father's father.
16	... ...	... ...	...	,, brother.
17	... ...	... ...	...	,, ,,
18	... ...	... ...	...	Sister's child.
TOTAL, 18	9	7	1	5

The questions connected with family predisposition and heredity of the disease will be again recurred to in reference to the lepers in general apart from the form of the disease.

The information attainable regarding the first symptoms of onset of the disease is like that regarding questions of age and time only worthy of quali-

Initial symptoms: eruption, fissures of the skin.

fied acceptance. In three cases the patients could give no account of the commencement of their malady; in 17 it is said to have been attended by the appearance of red patches of eruption on different parts of the body; in 5 by similar patches of a pale color; in 8 by patches of eruption accompanied by cracking of the heels; in 1 by eruption and the appearance of bullæ on the feet; in 5 by cracking of the soles of the feet; in 1 by pain and cracking of the skin over one ankle; in 3 by the appearance of bullæ on various parts of the body; in 2 by ulceration of the extremities; in 2 by the appearance of abscesses; in 1 by whitlow and necrosis of one of the fingers; in 1 by swelling and pain of the toes. If any conclusion is to be arrived at from these statements, it is that the commonest symptom attracting attention to the commencement of the disease is an eruption of some form, such having occurred, it is affirmed, in 31 of the 49 cases.

3.—*Analysis of the cases in the Asylum affected with the Tuberculated form of Leprosy.*

There were 12 cases, or 15·0 per cent. of the total cases, in which nodular appearances were by far the most prominent features in the disease.

Number of cases of tuberculated leprosy.

Of these ten were males and only two were females, or 21·7 per cent. and 5·8 per cent. respectively on the total lepers in the Asylum.

Distribution of the nodules.—In all these cases the face and ears were the seats of tubercular deposit. In all

Distribution of the deposit.

save two the deposit there was extensive, and exceeded that in other sites. In one only was tubercular deposit in the extremities the most conspicuous feature, and in another it was generally diffused over the body. In two cases the tongue was greatly invaded, and in many others it was more or less affected. In five cases the evidences of tubercular deposit were limited to the face and ears; in

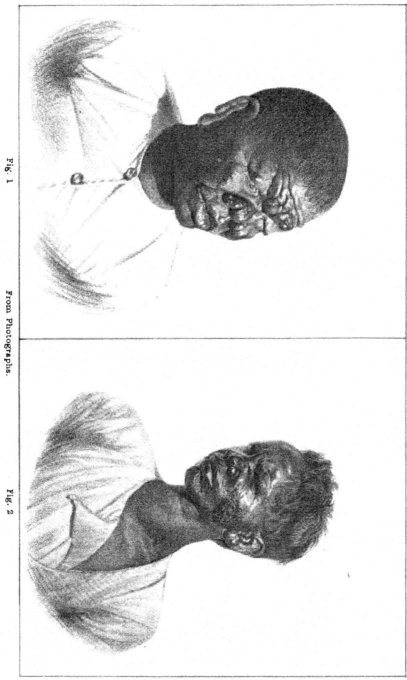

Fig. 1

From Photographs.

Fig. 2

TUBERCULATED FORM OF LEPROSY

Plate III.

the rest the extremities and other parts of the body participated to a greater or less extent.

The distribution of the deposit on the face, ears, &c.,
Manner in which the face and ears were affected.
varied greatly in different instances, and the manner in which it was deposited also exhibited considerable variety. In some cases it was diffused, causing general thickening over wide areas; in others it occurred as isolated, sharply-defined, prominent nodules. The sites of chief deposit were those well known as those specially selected in the disease—the malar prominences, eyebrows, nose and ears. In some cases there were prominent tubercles on the upper eyelids, which added considerably to the deformity due to the general thickening of the tissues and the coarse deep furrows on the forehead between the various areas of deposit. The deposit, when affecting the nose, generally appeared to take origin around three centres, affecting the tip and *alœ* respectively. This caused the formation of irregular lobes, and, when the condition was advanced, ended in causing the nose to present a distinct tri-lobed extremity. The lobes of the ears were very greatly affected, becoming thickened, nodular and pendulous, whilst smaller masses of deposit caused irregular roughening and thickening along the rims. The appearances present in advanced cases are very well shown in Plate III, Fig. 1, where the pendulous nodulated ears, the coarse folds on the forehead, the prominent tubercles on the upper eyelids, depressing them and almost closing the eyes, the general thickening of the cheeks, and the tri-lobed condition of the nose are all clearly visible.

Where tubercular deposits occurred in the extremities it
Tubercular deposit in the extremities.
was often difficult to determine to what extent they were due to deposit in the course of the cutaneous nerves, and how far to material actually occupying the tissue of the skin itself. Many of them were, however, so superficial, that if in any way specially connected with the nerves, it could only have been with their terminal filaments.

Anœsthesia.—In only one case did this appear to be
Presence of anæsthetic symptoms associated with the deposit.
entirely absent. This was an acute case of short duration; the patient was a boy of 10, and the disease had only lasted for one year. In the other

cases the areas occupied by deposit were more or less completely anæsthetic, but general anæsthesia of entire regions was much less common, complete, or extensive than in the form of the disease first described. When present, it showed the same preference for the extremities and for the extensor rather than the flexor surfaces of the affected limbs, as was previously noted in reference to anæsthetic leprosy (page 38).

In one case only was pain complained of. It extended across the dorsum of the right

Pain only present in one case.

foot from the fourth toe, which was distorted and swollen, to the inner side of the ankle joint.

Except over the sites of deposit, the skin of the patients as a rule presented no abnormal

Condition of the skin.

appearances. In two cases a scaly eruption was present, which in one covered the extremities and the lower portion of the trunk, and in the other was situated over the ankle joints. In five cases there were open ulcers on the feet or hands, in one there was also a large open ulcerating surface on the right cheek (Plate III, Fig. 2), and in another the tongue was ulcerated. In five cases the extremities were quite unaffected by ulceration, distortion, or absorptive changes of any kind; in the remaining seven there was more or less distortion or other evidence of a leprous affection.

The voice was affected in ten out of the twelve cases. Of the remaining two, one patient

Affection of the voice.

was dumb, the other was the boy previously mentioned as presenting no anæsthetic symptoms. The affection of the voice was probably due to tubercular deposit about the larynx, and was no doubt considerably influenced by the condition of the nose, which was sunken in five cases, and in others appeared to be so, due to the thickening and prominence of surrounding parts.

The ages of the patients ranged from 10 to 39 years, with an average of 27 years.

Ages of the cases.

The earliest date of attack was 9 years, the latest 30. Taking the eleven cases in regard to which information as to age could be obtained, one was attacked under 10 years of age, six between 10 and 20, three between 20 and 30, and one at 30. The average date of attack for the eleven cases is 18·90 years.

The duration of the disease varied from 1 to 14 years

Age of attack, and duration of disease. with an average of 8·27 for all cases. Of the cases eight had lasted for a period of under 10 years, and three for periods between 10 and 20 years.

In three, or 25 per cent. of the cases, there was a history

Leprosy among relatives. of the occurrence of leprosy in the patient's family; in the remaining eight the existence of disease among any relatives was denied. The affected relatives were in one case the father, in the second the mother, and in the third the mother's brother.

In eleven cases a history of the initial symptoms of the

Initial symptoms. disease was obtained. In seven the occurrence of patches of eruption is stated to have been the first symptom; in one cracking of the skin of the heels followed by eruption; in two cracking of the skin of the feet; in one a similar affection of the skin over the ankle joints; and in one generally diffused pain in the joints of the extremities. Here, as in the case of the anæsthetic form of the disease, eruption seems to have been the most common initial symptom.

The blood was examined microscopically in ten of the

The microscopical characters of the blood. twelve cases. In eight of these the number of white corpuscles present in the specimens was excessive. In some this excess was very strongly marked, and the normal white corpuscles were accompanied by an abundance of smaller bioplastic fragments. In two cases, the only abnormal feature present was a soft and adhesive condition of the red corpuscles—a condition which also occurred along with the excess of white corpuscles in one of the other cases.

4.—*Analysis of the cases in the Asylum affected equally by the Two forms of disease*—"Mixed" *Leprosy.*

"*Mixed*" *Leprosy.*—This variety of the disease occurred

Number of cases of Mixed Leprosy. in 15, or 18·6 per cent. of the total cases. It was in one or two cases a matter of doubt whether cases included under this head should not rather be referred to one or other of the previous categories, but with regard to all the rest there could be no doubt as to the propriety of retaining them in an intermediate class, as the tuberculated and anæsthetic phenomena were so equally balanced, that it was impossible to say which predominated.

From their very nature it necessarily follows that the variety in the symptoms was very great. In some the only feature distinguishing them from purely

Difficulty of separating such cases from the others.

anæsthetic cases was more or less distinct thickening of the alæ of the nose, or slight deposit about the cheeks and eyebrows, and in one specially doubtful case the tubercles were confined to the feet. The extent of anæsthesia also varied greatly. Special details in regard to these points are unnecessary, as they would in great part consist of repetitions of those previously given in connection with the tuberculated or anæsthetic cases. In one case the tongue was anæsthetic, but the sense of taste was partially retained.

In three cases the skin was manifestly more or less affected apart from the changes due to the presence of tuber-

Affection of the skin.

cular deposit. In one of these the skin of the face was shrivelled and presented a peculiar dried-up appearance; in another the skin about the knees was shrivelled, in coarse folds, and marked by scars, and in the third there was a white patch on the skin of one of the feet.

In seven cases active ulceration was present, in six of them confined to the extremities, and in one affecting the nose.

Presence of ulcers.

In three the toes showed degenerative changes in more or less marked degree, and in five there had been more or less complete loss of digits.

In seven cases the voice was affected, being husky to a greater or less degree, and in two the nose was sunken; in

Affection of the voice.

neither of these was there any discharge associated with the condition, nor was there any history of syphilis.

The cases consisted of eight males and seven females, or 17·3 per cent. and 20·5 per cent. respectively on the total male

Sex of the cases.

and female inmates of the Asylum.

The ages of the patients varied from 16 to 54, with an average 33·8 for the total. The date of attack varied from 3

Age of attack and duration of disease.

years to 40 years of age; five cases were attacked previous to 10 years of age; three between 10 and 20; two between 20 and 30; four between 30 and 40; one at 40. The average age of attack was 20·2 years. The duration of the disease ranged from 5 to 24 years; in four cases it was beneath 10 years; in eight, between 10 and 20 years; in three, between 20 and 30. The average duration was 13·66 years.

In six cases, or 40 per cent., there was a history of disease among the patients' relatives. In one both parents and four brothers were lepers, in two the father was a leper, in two the mother, and in one a son.

Leprosy among relatives.

In fourteen of the cases a history of the initial symptoms was obtained. In nine the disease was stated to have begun with eruption over more or less of the surface of the body; in one by the appearance of small tubercles, in one by the occurrence of a blister over one of the hip joints, in one by cracking of the skin of the soles of the feet, in one by a similar affection accompanied by thickening of the face, and in one by thickening of the ears.

Initial symptoms of the disease.

The blood was examined in 13 cases. In seven it appeared to be quite normal, in four the white corpuscles were present in excess; in one excess of white corpuscles was associated with an abundance of bioplastic fragments and a soft glutinous condition of the red corpuscles, and in one a similar condition of the red corpuscles was the only peculiarity. In one case bleeding occurred on the slightest irritation over the anæsthetic areas, and in another blood could only be obtained with difficulty.

Microscopical characters of the blood.

5.—*Analysis of cases in the Asylum in which the eruption was the most marked feature*—" Eruptive " *Leprosy.*

Although it is questionable whether this should be separated as a variety from one or other of the previous categories, seeing that the eruption seems rather to constitute a symptom common to the previous classes, there are, at the same time, certain cases in which this symptom is of such marked and persistent character as to justify their separation. Four cases of this kind were met with among the inmates of the Almora Asylum. Of these three were males and one a female.

Eruption rather an initial symptom than a special form of the disease.

G

In three of them the symptoms associated with the eruption were of a markedly anæsthetic nature, whilst in the fourth the anæsthesia was of very limited extent, and the eruption had a peculiar aspect, appearing rather to be due to diffuse tubercular deposits of minute size, varying from mere points to the size of sago-grains, than to an eruption of the nature ordinarily occurring as a symptom of leprosy. In the remaining cases the eruption consisted of irregularly rounded pale-colored patches, more or less symmetrically distributed (*vide* Plate I), and generally bounded by slightly elevated margins of a faint pinkish hue. The skin over such patches was, as a rule, more or less distinctly anæsthetic, and in one case progressive increase in the degree of anæsthesia could be clearly determined in proceeding from their margins towards the centres.

Eruption associated with marked anæsthetic symptoms in three cases.

As previously mentioned, anæsthesia was very extensive in three of the cases, affecting the face, the entire upper and lower extremities and portions of the trunk. In the fourth case it was confined to the extremities from the elbows and knees. In none of the cases were there any characteristic tubercular features present.

There were numerous scars along the extensor surface of the right upper extremity in two cases, and traces of burns on the hand of a third. The skin at the elbows in one and over the knees in another was dry, shrivelled, and thrown into coarse folds. Active ulceration existed in three cases; there was more or less absorption or loss of digits in all, and in two the remaining digits were strongly contracted.

Condition of the skin: presence of ulcers and loss of digits.

The blood was examined microscopically in three out of the four cases, and found to be perfectly normal in appearance.

Microscopical character of the blood.

The ages of the patients varied from 15 to 40, with an average of 30·25 years. The earliest age of attack was 8, the latest 31 years; one occurred previous to 10 years; one between 10 and 20; one between 20 and 30; and one at 31. The average for all cases was 20·25 years. The duration ranged from 5 to 16 years, that of two cases being beneath 10 years, that of the others between 10 and 20. The average was 10 years.

Age of attack, and duration of disease.

In one case the patient's mother and one brother were

lepers; in the rest the occurrence of leprosy among relatives was denied.

In two cases the disease was said to have begun with the

appearance of patches of eruption over the body, in one with cracking of the skin of the soles of the feet, and in one no history could be obtained.

6.—*Analysis of the features common to all the forms and varieties of Leprosy as observed in the Asylum.*

The foregoing chapters constitute a summary of the symptoms and history obtained by a

systematic examination of the various forms of leprosy in the Asylum, and we next proceed to consider some questions common to all of them as varieties of one disease.

The following table shows the age of attack of all cases in which information could be obtained on the point :—

TABLE 11.—*Showing the Age of Attack in all the forms of Leprosy.*

MALES.				FEMALES.			
Number of cases.	Age in years.	Number of cases.	Age in years.	Number of cases.	Age in years.	Number of cases.	Age in years.
5	8	3	28	1	8	2	20
2	9	8	30	1	8	3	22
2	10	2	31	3	9	4	25
1	11	1	82	1	11	6	80
8	12	1	88	1	12	1	81
1	13	1	36	1	13	1	32
1	14	1	88	2	16	1	33
2	16	3	40	1	17	1	37
4	18	1	47	1	18	1	58
3	24	1	50	1	19	1	60
2	25	1	58				
1	26						

The age of attack among the 79 cases varied from 3 to 60 years, the average being 23·73. The average age for males was 23·68, that for females 23·79.

Average age of attack of all cases:

The following statement shows the average age of attack in the four classes of cases compared with one another, and with the average for the total :—

And of the various forms compared.

TABLE 12.—*Average Age of Attack in each of the several forms of Leprosy.*

Total.	Anæsthetic cases.	Tubercular cases.	Mixed cases.	Eruptive cases.
23·73 years.	26·18 years.	18·90 years.	20·2 years.	20·25 years.

The next statement shows ages of attack according to decennial periods :—

Age of attack in decennial periods.

TABLE 13.—*Occurrence of Attack in Decennial periods.*

Decennial Periods.	Total Lepers.	Anæsthetic cases.	Tubercular cases.	Mixed cases.	Eruptive cases.
0 to 10 years ...	12	5	1	5	1
10 to 20 ,, ...	22	12	6	3	1
20 to 30 ,, ...	18	12	3	2	1
30 to 40 ,, ...	19	13	1	4	1
40 to 50 ,, ...	4	3	0	1	0
50 to 60 ,, ...	3	3	0	0	0
60 to 70 ,, ...	1	1			

The above figures, although obtained from a comparatively small number of cases, are generally in accordance with what has been recorded by other writers. The averages show that the average date of attack was latest in pure anæsthetic cases, earliest in those in which tubercular symptoms predominated, and, as might have been expected, intermediate

The figures obtained from the Almora Asylum generally agree with those from other sources:

for the mixed and eruptive cases. · The climax of anæsthetic cases occurred in the decennial period between 30 and 40, but the number of cases for the two preceding periods was almost equal to it, whilst that in the two following ones is less than a quarter as great, and is followed by the minimum in the next. In the tuberculated form, on the other hand, the maximum occurred in the second decennial period; the number furnished by the third is diminished by one-half, and is followed by the minimum in the fourth period. The mixed cases are more equally distributed, but the numbers show two maxima, one in the first, the other in the fourth period, probably indicating a division of the cases into two sections, one in which the anæsthetic, the other in which the tubercular element predominated. The four cases of eruptive leprosy are equally distributed over the first four decennial periods.

There is one point in which these figures regarding the age of attack do not correspond with those derived from some other sources, and this is that, in regard to average age of attack compared with sex, there is no evidence of a tendency to earlier attack in females than males. On the contrary, the average age for the females is slightly in excess of that for the males. That this average is not fallacious, but really corresponded with a greater tendency to early attack among the males, is shown by the following statement of numbers of attacks in the sexes according to decennial periods :—

But the average age of attack for females comes out as higher than that for males.

TABLE 14.—*Age of Attack in the Males and Females according to Decennial periods.*

Decennial Periods.				Percentage of Attacks at the different periods.	
				Male Lepers.	Female Lepers.
0 to 10 years	...	...	...	15·5	14·7
10 to 20 ,,	...	•••	...	31·1	23·5
20 to 30 ,,	...	...	...	20·0	26·4
30 to 40 ,,	...	•••	•••	20·0	29·4
40 to 50 ,,	...	•••	...	8·8	0·0
50 to 60 ,,	...	...	...	4·4	2·9
60 to 70 ,,	...	•••	...	0·0	2·9

The phenomenon in the present instance is no doubt in great measure due to the differences in the percentage of males and females suffering from anæsthetic and tuberculated leprosy, for the percentage of females for the former was 70·5, and that of the males was only 55·5, whilst the conditions were reversed in regard to tubercular leprosy, 20·0 per cent. of the males and only 5·8 per cent. of the females suffering from it. The average age of attack for females in the anæsthetic form was less than that for males, being 24·8 compared with 27·4, which tends to the same conclusion.

This probably due to small number of cases of tuberculated leprosy among the females in the Asylum.

The next table shows the duration of disease:

TABLE 15.—*Duration of Disease.*

MALES.				FEMALES.			
Number of cases.	Duration in years.	Number of cases.	Duration in years.	Number of cases.	Duration in years.	Number of cases.	Duration in years.
3	1	3	15	2	2	1	17
1	2	4	16	1	4	1	18
3	6	2	17	4	5	3	20
3	7	1	18	1	6	1	22
1	8	1	19	2	7	1	23
8	9	2	20	3	8	3	24
8	10	1	21	3	9	3	25
6	12	3	23	2	10	1	27
1	13	1	32	1	15	1	29
2	14	1	40				

The shortest period of duration was 1 year, the longest 40; the average for all cases was 13·69 years; the average duration for males was 13·66 and that for females 13·73 years.

Average duration of all cases.

The following are the average periods of duration in each form of disease compared with one another and with the total average:—

TABLE 16.—*Average Duration of the different forms of the Disease.*

AVERAGE DURATION OF THE DISEASE IN YEARS.

Total Lepers.	Anæsthetic cases.	Tubercular cases.	Mixed cases.	Eruptive cases.
13·69	15·22	8·27	13·66	10·0

The following table shows periods of duration according to decennial periods:—

TABLE 17.—*Duration of the several forms of Leprosy in Decennial Periods.*

Decennial periods.	Total cases.	Anæsthetic cases.	Tubercular cases.	Mixed cases.	Eruptive cases.
0 to 10 years	30	16	8	4	2
10 to 20 „	28	15	3	8	2
20 to 30 „	19	16	0	3	0
30 to 40 „	1	1	0	0	0
40 to 50 „	1	1	0	0	0

With regard to the question of duration, these figures are of course very insufficient, as they do not show duration to the termination of the disease, but only to time of examination.

The figures of duration only afford approximate information, due to absence of medical history for the Asylum.

Unfortunately, however, they constitute all the information which is at present attainable on the subject from the Almora Asylum. It is only quite recently that information regarding the date of attack has been registered, or that the cases have been discriminated according to the form of disease, so that nothing can be obtained from the past history of the institution. In the failure, then, of better evidence on the subject, we are driven to take the length of residence in the Asylum. There is no evidence to show that tubercular leprosy has latterly increased in frequency as compared with the anæsthetic form of the disease, so as to have caused the entrance of a disproportionate number of cases into the asylum within recent years, and none that there is a tendency among the sufferers from any special form of the disease to desert the institution, so that the average duration of cases at present in the Asylum probably represents the actual relations existing in this respect between the various forms of the disease. The want of previous records is more likely to give origin to serious fallacy in attempting to calculate the relative frequency of the occurrence of the different forms of disease, for those of the latter whose duration is longest are likely to furnish an accumulation of cases of survival giving rise to an appearance of relative prevalence greater than actually exists.

The figures as they stand advance evidence of their
Duration of tubercular leprosy much shorter than that of the anæsthetic form. correctness by agreeing with those obtained in other places in showing the much shorter duration of the tubercular as compared with the anæsthetic form.

In regard to the case with a duration of 40 years, it was very difficult to determine whether the patient was, at the time of examination, suffering from actual disease or only from the effects of that which had formerly been present; save slight ulceration of the soles of the feet, there were no symptoms but those ascribable to former nervous injury and muscular atrophy. The short duration of the eruptive cases corresponds with the initial character of the symptom as a manifestation of the disease.

7.—*The evidence which the Asylum affords on Contagion.*

The theory that leprosy is a contagious disease has in
Question relative to the contagiousness of leprosy. recent years been revived in some quarters, and a careful inquiry was therefore made for any evidence bearing on the point. The means which most naturally suggested itself for doing so was an examination of the history of all the married lepers, for were the result of this to show that the wives or husbands, as the case might be, of lepers, suffer frequently from the disease, this would be some evidence in favour of contagion, except in cases in which the marriage was demonstrated to be one contracted between lepers, or in which there was a family history of leprosy for both the contracting parties. Even with these limitations, evidence of this nature collected in a district in which leprosy is endemic would be by no means conclusive, as the possibility of remote hereditary taint or even of *de novo* development of the disease would remain. In the present instance, as will be seen, we are fortunately not obliged to enter into such considerations.

The following statement shows the numbers of male and female married lepers, and of the condition of their husbands and wives :

TABLE 18.—*Condition of Wives and Husbands of Married Lepers.*

MALES.					FEMALES.				
	STATE OF WIFE.					STATE OF HUSBAND.			
Number.	Alive or Dead.	Leprous.	Non-Leprous.	REMARKS.	No.	Alive or Dead.	Leprous.	Non-Leprous.	REMARKS.
1	Alive ...	0	1		1	Alive ...	0	1	
2	,, ...	0	1		2	,, ...	0	1	Married as a child.
3	,, ...	0	1		3	Dead ...	0	1	Ditto ditto.
4	,, ...	0	1		4	Alive ...	0	1	
5	,, ...	1	0	Married to a leper-woman in Asylum.	5	,, ...	0	1	
					6	2, 1st alive, 2nd dead.	1	1	2nd marriage in Asylum.
6	Dead ...	1	...	Ditto ditto.					
7	Alive ...	1	...	Ditto ditto.	7	2, 1st alive, 2nd dead.	1	1	Ditto ditto.
8	,, ...	0	1		8	2, both alive...	1	1	Ditto ditto.
9	,, ...	0	1		9	Dead ...	0	1	
10	,, ...	0	1		10	1 Alive ...	0	1	
					11	Alive ...	1	0	Married in Asylum.
11	,, ...	1	0	Ditto ditto.	12	2, 1st alive, 2nd dead.	1	1	2nd marriage in Asylum.
12	,, ...	0	1		13	2 Alive. ...	1	1	Ditto ditto.
13	1 alive, 2 dead.	0	3	Thrice married, all wives non-leprous.	14	Ditto ...	1	1	Ditto ditto.
					15	Alive ...	0	1	
14	1 Ditto	0	1		16	Dead ...	1	0	
15	1 alive, 1 dead.	1	1	1st wife alive, 2nd marriage in Asylum.	17	,, ...	0	1	
					18	Alive ...	0	1	
16	Alive ...	0	1		19	,, ...	0	1	
17	Dead ...	0	1		20	,, ...	0	1	
18	Alive ...	0	1		21	Dead ...	0	1	
19	,, ...	1	0	Married in Asylum.	22	2 Alive ...	1	1	2nd marriage in Asylum.
20	,, ...	1	0	Ditto ditto.	23	Dead ...	0	1	
21	Dead ...	0	1		24	2 Alive ...	1	1	Ditto ditto.
22	Alive ...	0	1		25	Dead ...	0	1	
23	,, ...	0	1		26	Alive ...	0	1	
24	,, ...	0	1		27	Dead ...	0	1	
25	,, ...	1	0	Ditto ditto.					
TOTAL 25		8	20	The eight lepers were married in Asylum.	27		10	25	Nine out of the ten leprous husbands were married in Asylum.

H

Of the 52 lepers married, 18 had leprous wives or husbands, but as 17 of these marriages were contracted between lepers in the Asylum, there remains only 1 case in which the possibility of contagion is to be considered, and certainly this isolated instance cannot be regarded as affording any trustworthy evidence, as in an endemic area the possibility of the occasional occurrence of marriages between predisposed parties must always exist.

No facts ascertained in the history of the lepers favouring a belief in the contagious nature of the disease.

The history of the Asylum furnishes no other evidence in favour of contagion; there is no evidence of attendants or others employed about the institution or of those in any way connected with it having suffered from the discharge of their duties in any way.*

No evidence afforded by the history of the Asylum.

8.—*The evidence which the histories of the inmates afford on the influence of heredity.*

We next come to the question of heredity of the disease. The inmates of this Asylum belonging to more or less localised hill communities offer greater facilities for the elucidation of this subject than the inmates of similar asylums in the plains, seeing that the former have usually more definite information than the latter concerning their present and ancestral relatives. On this account, therefore, the information which we have obtained from these people regarding the influence of heredity in the propagation of leprosy may, we think, be considered as of more than ordinary trustworthiness.

---

* Among the cases reported to the College of Physicians in support of the contagious nature of the disease, there is one quoted on the authority of a Native Sub-Assistant Surgeon, in which it is stated that two men, who acted as durwans, *i. e.*, gate-keepers, at the Almora Asylum, were attacked by leprosy whilst so employed. ["Report on Leprosy by the Royal College of Physicians"; London, 1867—page 141.]

On referring to the Superintendent of the Institution, the Rev. Mr. Budden, for information on the point, we have been informed that the Sub-Assistant Surgeon in question "knew nothing about the Asylum; and the statement," writes Mr. Budden, "has no foundation whatever. Nothing of the kind reported has ever occurred in the Asylum since I took charge of it in 1851."

TABLE 19.—*Lepers with Leprous Relatives.*

Number.	PARENTS.			Brothers.	Sisters.	Sons.	Daughters.	Other Relations.		Total Relations affected with Leprosy.
	Both.	Father.	Mother.							
1	1	...	...	4	...	...	...	...	...	6
2	1	...	...	...	...	...	...	...	...	2
3	1	...	...	...	...	...	...	...	...	2
4	1	...	...	3	...	...	...	...	...	5
5	...	1	...	...	...	...	...	...	...	1
6	...	1	...	...	...	...	...	...	...	1
7	...	1	...	...	...	...	...	...	...	1
8	...	...	1	...	1	...	...	...	...	2
9	...	...	1	...	...	...	...	...	...	1
10	...	...	1	...	...	...	...	...	...	1
11	...	...	1	...	...	...	...	...	...	1
12	...	...	1	...	...	...	...	...	...	1
13	...	...	1	1	...	...	...	Mother's brother	...	3
14	...	...	1	...	...	...	...	...	...	1
15	...	...	1	1	...	...	...	Mother's brother	...	3
16	...	...	1	...	...	...	...	...	...	1
17	...	...	1	...	...	...	...	...	...	1
18	...	...	...	...	...	...	...	Father's brother	...	1
19	...	...	...	...	...	...	...	Ditto	...	1
20	...	...	...	...	...	...	...	Mother's brother	...	1
21	...	...	...	...	...	...	...	Father's father	...	1
22	...	...	...	...	...	...	...	Sister's child	...	1
23	...	...	...	1	...	...	...	...	...	1
24	...	...	...	1	...	...	...	...	...	1
25	...	...	...	1	...	...	...	...	...	1
26	...	...	...	1	1	...	...	...	...	2
27	...	...	...	...	...	4	...	...	...	4
28	...	...	...	...	...	1	...	...	...	1
Total ... 28	4	3	10	13	2	5	...	7		48

The preceding table shows the number of lepers with leprous relatives, with the degree of relationship in each instance.

We thus obtain unequivocal information that of the 80 lepers in the Asylum at present, 28, or 35 per cent., had one or more leprous relatives. This percentage gives a proportion 140 times greater than the percentage of lepers to the total population of the district, and allowing the fullest play to the possible influence of similarity of external conditions, points to the distribution of the disease by families and therefore to hereditary predisposition. The circumstance that in 2 of the 4 cases in which both parents were leprous, the total number of leprous relatives was greater than in any of the others, and in fact furnished nearly a fourth of the total of leprous relatives for the 28 cases, also supports this conclusion.

Percentage of cases with leprous relatives.

It should be borne in mind, moreover, that many of the inmates had not for years past learnt anything of the individual histories of the various members of their families, so that this circumstance (in addition to the paucity of precise information regarding the particular ailments of distant relatives, common to all families) tends to show that even this high ratio under-states the actual proportion of leprous kindred.

The figures in the table seem to indicate that there is a strongly marked tendency in the disease to follow the female line of descent. Of the 17 persons born of leprous parents, both parents were affected in 4 instances. The father alone was leprous in 3, whereas the mother alone was leprous in no less than 10—giving percentages of 23·5, 17·6, and 58·8 respectively on the total 17 cases. Taking all cases in which parents or parents' relatives are affected, we find 10 cases in which the father or father's relatives are leprous, and 17 in which the disease was present on the maternal side.

Tendency of the disease to follow the female line of descent.

Nineteen of the 28 cases with leprous relatives were males and 9 females. Of the former there were 9 cases in which the father or father's relatives were affected, 12 in which the mother or mother's relatives, 7 cases in which brothers', and 2 cases in which a sister or sister's relatives were leprous: among the latter, the father was affected in 1 instance, the mother in 5, a brother and sister in 1 and a son in 1; among the males, there were 15 cases in which male relatives and 10 in which

Sex of cases with leprous relatives compared with sex of such relatives.

female relatives were affected. Among the female lepers, on the other hand, there were 4 cases in which male and 6 in which female relatives were affected. The above figures are too limited in amount to form definite conclusions from, but they suggest the possibility of the existence of a tendency in the disease to adhere by preference to one or other sex in a leprous family.

Conditions favouring the development of the disease a subject for further investigation.

The special conditions favouring the development of the disease in the pre-disposed is a matter for further inquiry. The data attainable from the examination of the inmates of the Asylum did not throw much light on the point. The disease, so far as can be judged from these cases, would not appear to be specially prevalent among any particular class of the community, as is shown in the following statement :—

TABLE 20.—*Leprosy in relation to Caste.*

Leprosy considered in reference to caste and occupation.

Caste.	No. of cases in the Asylum.
Dome ...	39
Rájpút ...	30
Brahman ...	1
Buniyah ...	1
Christian ...	1

As the inhabitants of Kumaun virtually consist of two classes only—Rájpúts and Domes, the former representing an Aryan population, the latter the aboriginal people—whilst other classes are only very sparingly represented, the evidence, such as it is, is in favour of impartial distribution of the disease.*

The question of the influence of occupation in connection with the etiology of leprosy will be considered on a future occasion.

9.—The number of Children born in the Asylum, in connection with the statistics of the disease in the District.

Number and condition of children of lepers in the Asylum.

In connection with the question of heredity, and more especially in regard to the risk of an increase of the leper population of a district, the number and condition of the children of the lepers in the

* According to the Census Report of the North-West Provinces (1873) the composition of the Hindu population of the district of Kumaun in regard to caste is as follows :—
Brahmans (a) 25·4; Rájpúts 42·6; Buniyahs 0·8; other Hindu castes 31·2=100.
(a) "Among the lower ranks of Brahmans, great latitude is taken in regard to labour, food, &c., and their claim to the distinction of that caste is, in consequence, little recognised; the mass of the labouring population from similar causes have still less pretension to the designation of Rájpúts which they assume. The Domes are, of course, outcasts, and to them are left the whole of the inferior trades,—those of carpenters, masons, blacksmiths, miners, musicians, &c.,—and by them also are performed the most menial offices."—"Statistical Sketch of Kumaun," by G. W. Traill.—*Asiatic Researches,* Vol. XVI.

Asylum was carefully enquired into. The following table
is a summary of the information thus obtained:—

TABLE 21.—*Table showing the condition of the Children (101) of 51 of
the leprous inmates of the Asylum.*

No. of leper-parent.	MALES.		No. of leper-parent.	FEMALES.	
	Number of children.	Condition of children.		Number of children.	Condition of children.
1	1	Healthy ; alive.	1	1	Healthy.
2	1	„ „	2	0	
3	0	... ...	3	0	
4	2	1 dead.	4	0	
5	2	Alive ; healthy. Born in Asylum.	5	0	
6	2	1 dead ; 1 alive, healthy. By marriage in Asylum.	6	2	Dead. By marriage at home.
7	0	... ...	7	1	Healthy. Born in Asylum.
8	1	Alive ; healthy.	8	2	Healthy ; 1 born in Asylum, 1 at home.
9	3	„ „	9	6	2 dead, 4 healthy.
10	1	Dead.	10	7	5 dead ; all born at home
11	0	... ...	11	0	1 dead ; all born at home ; 4 healthy.
12	3	Alive ; healthy.	12	5	Healthy.
13	0	... ...	13	0	7 dead.
14	2	Alive ; healthy.	14	1	4 leprous. Husband a leper.
15	1	Dead.	15	8	Healthy.
16	4	Healthy.	16	9	4 dead, 4 healthy.
17	1	„	17	2	1 „ 1 „
18	1	„	18	8	1 „ 4 „
19	0	...	19	2	3 „ 2 „
20	0	...	20	5	Dead.
21	0	... ...	21	5	Healthy.
22	0	... ...	22	3	
23	1	Healthy.	23	1	
24	1	„	24	0	
25	0	... ...	25	2	1 dead, 1 alive ; healthy.
			26	4	Healthy.
			27	2	1 leprous.
TOTAL 25	27	23 alive—0 leprous, 4 dead.	27	76	46 alive—5 leprous, 30 dead.

From this table we learn that the 52 married lepers in the Asylum have produced a total of 101 children. The numbers as stated in the table are 103, but a deduction of two has to be made, as two are entered in both columns, being the offspring of marriages in the Asylum. Of these 69 are alive. These 52 lepers have contributed a permanent addition of 17, or 32·6 per cent., to the population under review; for 52 of the children must be deducted as merely replacing their parents, so that the possible increase of lepers due to them is 17. It is, however, extremely unlikely that all the children should live, or that all that live should turn out leprous, so that the probability of actual increase is almost *nil*. The foregoing table shows, that the mortality among the offspring of lepers is very high. 39·4 per cent. of the children of female lepers is seen to have succumbed at an early age, or 33·6 per cent., when the mortality of the juvenile offspring of both the male and the female lepers is estimated; it is therefore probable that a considerable proportion of those still living will be short-lived. Up to the present time only 5 cases of leprosy have manifested themselves among the children, and of these 1 is dead, so that only 4 of the leper parents have been substituted as yet by leper children, leaving an excess of 48 to be accounted for. The proportion of lepers among these children is very small, which is probably due to the fact that many of them are still beneath the age at which the disease usually manifests itself. At the same time many others are adults, manifest no indications of leprosy, are married, and have apparently healthy children.

Amount of increase possible in leprous population due to the lepers in the Asylum.

Our figures seem to suggest that another fact should be taken into consideration in endeavouring to estimate the risk of increase in the leper population, and this is the very small number of children produced by the majority of the leprous parents.

Total number of children very small.

In connection with this point, it is very remarkable to observe how much smaller a number of children is to be credited to the male than to the female lepers, the absolute numbers being 27 and 76 respectively, and the averages of children to families being 1·08 in one case and 2·8 in the

Of these cases the females contribute a much larger number of children than the males.

other, or after deducting those cases in which both parents
were lepers, 1·0 and 2·8 respectively. A third of the 27
male married lepers have no offspring. So far as the evidence goes, the total number contributed to the population
by the female lepers is about 70 per cent. in excess of that
contributed by the males. As a set-off to this, however, the
table shows that about 24 per cent. more of the children born
to female lepers died than of the children born to male lepers.

If the figures really mean the actual occurrence of
larger families where the female than where the male
parent is leprous, several explanations of the phenomenon
suggest themselves. It appears probable that the age at
which the disease is developed exerts an important influence.
It cannot, however, act directly to any great extent, for, as
a general rule, we know that the disease tends to be developed as soon, if not sooner, in the female than in the male.
It is the inequality in the age of the parents which appears
likely to tell on the number of children. In this country
there is often such great disparity between the ages of men
and their wives that, allowing the age for the manifestation
of disease to be practically alike for both, the females
have a much longer time previous to its advent in which to
produce children than the males have.

That the age of manifestation of the disease really does
influence the numbers of chil-
Probable explanation of this fact; dren in one way or other is supported by the facts recorded in the following table, which
shows the ages at which the parents became leprous and
the numbers of children in the family. The cases of leper-
marriages in the Asylum have been excluded, as well as one
in which the age of attack in the parent was unknown :—

TABLE 22.—*Age of attack, and number of Children of Married Lepers*

MALES.				FEMALES.			
Age of attack (years).	No. of children.	Age of attack (years).	No. of children.	Age of attack (years).	No. of children.	Age of attack (years).	No. of children.
24	1	32	2	16	0	30	8
25	1	38	0	19	0	30	8
25	0	40	0	22	0	30	5
26	1	40	0	22	0	30	1
28	4	40	3	22	1	31	4
30	1	47	1	25	2	32	2
30	1	50	3	25	2	35	2
31	2	58	1	30	5	58	5
						60	9

The chief interest connected with these figures lies in the fact that they appear to supply a means of, in a great degree, explaining, for this country at all events, the apparent preference of the disease to follow the female line of descent. The tendency to follow the female line is possibly, however, also, partially due in many districts, such as Kumaun, to the greater frequency of the tuberculated form of leprosy among males than females—that form usually appearing at an earlier age than the anæsthetic.

and of the tendency in the disease to follow the female line of descent.

Returning to the question of increase in the leper population, we must, in order to arrive at any definite conclusion, endeavour to obtain further information as to the number of children born in other leper families and the proportion of them who become leprous. The only data at our disposal in the present instance consist of those furnished by the family history of those of the lepers whose parents were leprous. Seventeen such cases exist, and the particulars of these are embodied below :—

Further data regarding increase in leper population.

TABLE 23.—*Table showing the number of Children and of Leprous Children in 17 Families in which one or both Parents were leprous.*

No.	Parents.	No. of children.	No. of leprous children.
1	Both.	10	5
2	,,	3	1
3	,,	4	1
4	,,	7	4
5	Father.	2	1
6	,,	5	1
7	,,	5	1
8	Mother.	3	2
9	,,	2	2
10	,,	3	2
11	,,	4	1
12	,,	2	1
13	,,	2	1
14	,,	4	1
15	,,	2	1
16	,,	6	1
17	,,	4	1
17	21	63	27

K

We have here 17 leprous families containing 21 leprous parents giving 68 children, of whom 27 are leprous. This is a larger proportion of children, and

Facts obtained from the family history of the inmates of the Asylum.

a very much larger proportion of leprous children, than is given by the other set of cases (Table 21), where, reckoning all those cases in which those married are both lepers, and allowing for the cases apppearing in both columns, we have 52 lepers with 101 children, and 5 leprous children. The numerical data before us, illustrating the extent to which a manifestly leprous parent may determine the predisposition to the disease in his own immediate offspring, may be thus summarised :—To 79 leprous persons 169 children were born ; 34 of these are known to have died prematurely. Among the remaining 135 children leprosy has already manifested itself in 32 cases, or in 23·7 per cent., nearly one-fourth of the total number. This, too, doubtless materially understates the number of cases of the disease which may ultimately occur among them, as the majority of the children are below the average age at which the disease manifests itself. Nevertheless, when we take into consideration the comparatively small families which lepers have and the high rate of mortality among the children, it is not probable that the contribution to the leprous community will in the present instance do more than replace the numbers of the present generation. Indeed, the figures which are before us may be worked out to show an actual decrease, but we consider the number of cases with regard to which we possess accurate information too small to form the ground of practical generalisations.

Taking all the information attainable from these figures, there appears, therefore, to be no great risk of increase to the leper population of Kumaun as

The risk of increase in the leper population of Kumaun, small.

far as the disease is dependent on heredity for its multiplication.

Since the year 1866, from which period only trustworthy data are available from the registers of the Asylum, 7 births have occurred in the institution.

Very small number of births occurring in the Asylum.

The total number of inmates of the Asylum during the period have been 114 males and 61 females; and as until the present year there has been no attempt at separation of the sexes beyond giving them separate sleeping compartments, and no supervision specially designed with the object of keeping them apart, the very small ratio of births is very remarkable, and must mainly, at all events, be credited to the influence of the disease. Between 1866 and 1871, moreover, 31 marriages were contracted between male and female lepers under the sanction of those in charge of the institution. In 29 of these marriages no children were produced; two were fruitful to the extent of two children each.

In connection with this subject, a very interesting experiment is now in progress at Almora. There are at present in the orphanage 12 children of lepers now or formerly inmates of the Asylum. The total number of such children who have been admitted into the orphanage is 14, but of these 1 has died, and another, a girl of 22, has now left the orphanage, is married and has children —healthy to all appearances. Of the 12 remaining, 7 were born in the Asylum of two leprous parents, 5, the offspring of one leprous and one healthy parent, were born in the villages to which their parents belonged. Their ages range from 19 to 5 years; their health and general condition is excellent, and as yet they show no signs of leprosy. The experiment is as yet imperfect, but it is capable of affording very valuable information if the future history of the children be carefully noted. They have been removed from the surroundings under which the disease manifested itself in their parents, have been well fed and carefully attended to, and their subsequent history cannot but throw light on the extent to which the influence of heredity can exert itself, or may be modified and kept in abeyance by ameliorated conditions of life.

Facts regarding the children of the inmates of the Asylum.

10.—*Practical suggestions.*

So far as our information goes, it appears then, that, even allowing for a certain proportion of imported cases, any risk of rapid increase in the prevalence of leprosy in Kumaun is not to be apprehended. We have no satisfactory evidence of contagion and none of a rapid *increase* of cases due to hereditary influences. Whilst, however, the prevalence of the disease remains as high as it is, there is ample reason for determined effort to

The prevalence of the disease so great as to deserve serious attention.

ascertain by what laws this prevalence is regulated and by what practical measures it may be diminished.

The means for effecting this can hardly be looked for in attempts at forcible repression of the disease, such as the compulsory imprisonment of lepers in Asylums. Quite apart from objections founded on the tyranny involved in any such measures, there are other serious and almost insurmountable difficulties in carrying them effectually out. It would not be sufficient merely to confine those suffering from developed disease, but all those who might in any degree be supposed to be hereditarily disposed towards it, would have also to be secured. It would, in truth, be even more important to secure the latter, for, from the present evidence, there appears to be only a very small number of children born to confirmed lepers. But had all those predisposed to be secured, how and by whom could the existence of predisposition be determined? In the case of hereditary predisposition, it is quite uncertain for how long—for how many generations, the disposition may be transmitted without giving any ostensible sign of its presence, but capable under certain circumstances of giving origin to the development of disease. How, then, is the absence or disappearance of predisposition to be determined?

Compulsory confinement of the leprous population not an efficient or practicable means of diminishing the prevalence of the disease.

That Asylums, properly so called, are very useful and desirable institutions in districts where chronic diseases like leprosy prevail, is just as true as that prisons ought not to be substituted for them. By their means a shelter is secured for the patients where they may be benefited by treatment, and where they, in many cases, are certainly saved from much suffering; where the phenomena of disease may be studied, and the effects of curative means tested. By their means, moreover, the existence of a large amount of miserable beggary in a district may be avoided. Such institutions are, beyond doubt, calculated to do very great good, and deserve all support and encouragement so long as such support does not relieve the relatives of the diseased from the performance of their duties to the sick—so long as their existence does not afford an encouragement to people to profit by the misfortune of their relatives at the expense of the community.

Benefits of Asylums as contrasted with prisons.

Such have been the results of our investigation during the present year. They have, at all events, served to clear the way for further work, and to point out the direction to be followed in more detailed local enquiry.*

---

* The results of our enquiries hitherto regarding leprosy correspond closely with a similar enquiry very recently carried out in Sicily by Dr. Profeta. We have already, in an earlier part of this Report, referred to this investigation, but as we have not seen any account of these researches in any English journal, we subjoin a short translated abstract of Dr. Profeta's paper. Since the year 1867, the author has collected information regarding 114 cases of leprosy in Sicily— 80 men and 34 women. In three-fourths of the cases he was able to trace the disease to inheritance—in a few instances he had to trace the malady in relatives four times removed. In no instance was there any evidence of contagion, although 22 of the lepers had lived with their families for many years.

Summary of results of a leprosy enquiry in Sicily.

Children who had been suckled by leprous women had not, apparently, been infected thereby, nor had re-vaccination with lymph obtained from leprous persons been shown to transmit the disease. (It is not mentioned how long a period has since elapsed.) The inference that leprosy may be dependent in some way on a fish diet is not (as mentioned in a previous page) supported by experience in Sicily, seeing that the disease prevails among the inland population to a greater extent than along the coast; nor do poverty, want, and filth seem to exercise important influence as factors, for the disease is even more prevalent among the well-to-do classes; and, least of all, could the disease be attributed to malarial influences. So that the author has come to the conclusion that heredity is the only ascertained etiological agent in its propagation —"So dass in der That nur die Erblichkeit als ätiologisches Moment übrig bleibt."

Of the 114 persons, 9 were affected at ages ranging from 7 to 10 years; 26, at 11 to 20 years; 39, at 21 to 30 years; 22, at 31 to 40 years; 11, at 41 to 50 years; and in 7 cases the disease was not manifested until the persons had reached ages ranging from 51 to 65 years. The duration of the disease, taking the average of all the cases, was 13 years, the minimum being 3 years and the maximum 40. Both the tuberculated and anæsthetic forms of leprosy occur in Sicily, the latter form being somewhat more common than the former.—Virchow and Hirsch's *Jahresbericht über die gesammten Medicin.*—X. Jahrgang, Band I. Abth. 2. S. 431 : Berlin, 1876.

SUMMARY.

A BRIEF recapitulation of the principal points to which reference has been made in this our first report regarding leprosy may be of use to such readers as have not sufficient time to study the question in detail. It must, however, be premised that any digest relating to such an obscure subject is necessarily attended with more risk of misinterpretation than a detailed report where all the qualifying circumstances of any set of deductions can be produced.

It will have been seen that although leprosy was known to prevail in Hindostan many centuries before the Christian era, comparatively little was known regarding its precise localisation in the different provinces until the general census of 1872 was taken. Not only was the comparative prevalence of the disease in various districts all over British India ascertained at that period, but the possibility of attaining to something approaching to a fair estimate of the aggregate leprous population of the country also became practicable. According to these census returns, there are some 99,000 lepers in the territories under British rule, yielding a proportion of 54 lepers to every 100,000 of the entire population, or (taking the actual figures in the first Table) 1 leper to every 1,845 persons. Of the aggregate number about one-eighth is contributed by certain districts, each of not less than 100,000 in population, furnishing a ratio nearly five times higher than the average ratio for the whole of India. In these districts there is a leper to every 384 persons instead of to 1,845. Should these latter data be verified on more close observation, an important step will have been made towards solving the difficulty of dealing with the question in a practical manner, as such a phenomenon must depend either on peculiar local or hereditary conditions.

Leprosy statistics of British India.

The leprosy statistics of specially affected districts.

One of these abnormally affected localities forms the subject of a special report on this occasion, *viz.*, the District of Kumaun. Roughly speaking, it contains 1,000 lepers. This yields a proportion equivalent to something over 250 per 100,000 of the population, or, calculating on the actual

The leprosy statistics of Kumaun.

figures of the estimate, 1 leper to about every 388 individuals (*vide* Table 5, page 22). With the object of mitigating the sufferings of at least a portion of this unfortunate class, the Commissioner, Sir Henry Ramsay, has founded an asylum at Almora with accommodation for over a hundred lepers.

The inmates of this Asylum formed the subject of a

Observations made at the Almora Leper Asylum. series of clinical observations, the details of which are recorded in the foregoing pages.

Eighty lepers were subjected to the closest scrutiny; 49

The forms of leprosy encountered. proved to be cases in which anæsthesia presented the most prominent feature; 12 in which the presence of tubercles in the skin was the most marked peculiarity; in 15 cases the two former conditions were so equally evident that they were classified as "mixed;" and in 4 cases an eruption formed the most pronounced symptom. The ratios which these yield agree generally with the proportion in which the different varieties of the disease have been observed to occur in other countries.

The average age at which the onset of the disease was

The age of attack and the duration of the disease. observed was found to be between 23 and 24 years; even the decimals obtained by calculating averages in the case of male and female lepers were found to be almost identical. There was, however, a range of from 3 years to 60. The average duration of the disease was nearly 14 years. The form in which anæsthesia was the prevailing feature was the most chronic, the average duration of the "tuberculated" cases being shorter by nearly six years.

The history of the Asylum gives no support to the doc-

The question of contagion. trine that leprosy is a contagious disease, but strong evidence to the contrary. The reverse has been stated with regard to the history of the Asylum, but it will have been seen, from the information elicited, that not the slightest foundation existed for such a statement.

But with reference to the probable influence of heredity

The influence of heredity. in the propagation of leprosy, the facts elicited, and which may, we believe, be accepted as trustworthy, give forth no uncertain sound. There can, we think, be no very substantial argument adduced in the face of the figures which have been collected in connection with this Asylum alone to contra-indicate the inference that hereditary taint exercises a most important influence in the transmission of the pest.

Taking into consideration, therefore, the prominent part undoubtedly played by heredity, and the fact that the disease but seldom manifests itself until after puberty, it is evident that any attempt at "stamping it out" by the compulsory segregation of leprous persons would prove wholly impracticable; for, as mentioned in the last chapter, it would not only be necessary to segregate those suffering from developed disease, but also those hereditarily disposed to it. How, and by whom, could the predisposition be determined? It would, indeed, be even more important to secure the latter class and such persons as are only mani-festly affected to a slight extent; for it would appear that persons of this description furnish by far the greater portion of the children who are, so to speak, potentially leprous,—time and circumstance alone being required for the develop-ment of the disease.

Compulsory segregation of le-pers impracticable.

In intimate relation with this question is that of the probability or otherwise of an increase in the prevalence of the disease amongst such a leprous community as exists in Kumaun. Fortunately it would appear that, *pari passu*, with the active manifestation of the disease, a tendency to sterility is also induced; moreover, the mortality among the children of lepers (even among such of them as are born before leprosy has manifested itself in the parents) appears to be abnormally high, so that the probable aggregate of the number of the offspring of lepers is to a very appreciable degree less than that furnished by non-leprous individuals. It is therefore evident that unless there be influences other than heredity at work in the locality tending towards the production of the leprous condition, no serious increment need be apprehended. It will be our en-deavour to ascertain on a future occasion whether any such leprosy-inducing conditions can be detected in the specially affected localities.

Regarding the factors in the maintenance of leprosy in parts of Kumaun.

With regard to the latter, we have drawn attention to the fact that the malady is far more prevalent along the Nepal frontier, a country in which a very large proportion of lepers are found, and it is believed that no organised attempt of any kind exists in it to relieve their sufferings. Indeed, the reverse is not uncommonly stated. Under these circumstances it is, perhaps, not strange that these districts should be exceptionally afflicted, especially when it is considered that the records of the Almora Leper Asylum show that one-fifth of the total number of the inmates who have received shelter since the institution was established have come from Nepal.

We may find that personal examination into the facts along these specially affected border parganas will dispel the plausibility of such an inference, but at present we are inclined strongly to attribute the exceptional prevalence of cases of leprosy in this part of Kumaun in a great measure to its having to give shelter to more than its own share of lepers—to support more, in fact, than is contributed to the population by its own quota of leprous stock.

We have abstained from making any observations regarding the pathology of leprosy on the present occasion. It will be more convenient to describe this portion of the inquiry when our microscopical investigations of the diseased tissue have been completed. These, for the greater part, we propose to carry out in Calcutta, where the Leper Asylum and the hospitals offer peculiar facilities for prosecuting researches of this character.

CALCUTTA,
November 1876.

CPSIA information can be obtained
at www.ICGtesting.com
Printed in the USA
BVOW09s1147050417
480379BV00008B/107/P